LOOKIN

How do you plot the best career path? How do you know you're heading in the right direction professionally? How do you effectively make a shift into a new industry about which you have little knowledge or experience? *Looking Beyond the Car in Front*, written by leading recruitment expert Grant Duncan, guides both senior and mid-career business executives in taking a more assertive and strategic longer-term approach to career choices. No other careers book includes insights from so many people who have steered their careers to the top of their professions.

The professional journey we're on is typically the result of a mixture of hard work, good luck, and brainpower, but not always proactive choices and decisions. Drawing on 40 years' experience of working with, talking to, and assessing executives with many different career journeys, the book offers an approach to set a longer-term mindset and a toolkit to help those who are thinking about their future career plans and, particularly, a career change. Grant has worked alongside some of the most successful business leaders, and the book offers unique insights from interviews with CEOs, successful entrepreneurs, and public and not-for-profit leaders from multiple sectors, including Roger Davis, Chairman of BUPA, Stevie Spring, Chairman of the British Council, Mind and Co-op NED, Stephen Carter, Informa plc Chair, Tim Davie, BBC Director General, and Alan Jope, Unilever plc CEO.

When following the car in front may seem the easiest, safest, and most rational course of action, it will not necessarily take you in the right direction. This book provides the perfect "front-seat navigator" in steering your next career move and for those supporting career development, including HR directors, coaches, and career management consultants.

Grant Duncan is Managing Director, Media, Entertainment, and Digital at global leadership advisory consultancy, Korn Ferry. He has 40 years of business experience gained in two professions. Grant's first career saw him rise to leadership roles in a number of UK advertising agencies, latterly as CEO of Publicis. His second career has been in executive recruitment, initially at global executive search firm, Spencer Stuart, before joining Korn Ferry.

"A well-written and highly useable take on how to take control of a career and maximise potential, illustrated by fascinating interviews with leading executives which bring this vividly to life."
— **William Eccleshare**, *Worldwide CEO of Clear Channel Outdoor Holdings, Inc*

"A practical and thoughtful career progression manual, rich in analysis, action-oriented advice and sound common sense."
— **Dame Cilla Snowball**, *Governor at Wellcome Trust, Director at Genome Research Ltd (Wellcome Sanger Institute), Non Executive Director Derwent London plc*

"A genuinely insightful guide to help people approach their career choices in a more proactive way, combining a playbook of techniques with the real-world journeys of senior executives."
— **Gavin Patterson**, *President and Chief Revenue Officer, Salesforce*

"A very practical and highly readable guide to career planning by a recognised leadership practitioner and thought-leader."
— **Stevie Spring** *CBE, Chairman of The British Council*

LOOKING BEYOND THE CAR IN FRONT

A GUIDE TO MAKING THE RIGHT CAREER CHOICES AT THE RIGHT TIME

Grant Duncan

LONDON AND NEW YORK

First published 2022
by Routledge
2 Park Square, Milton Park, Abingdon, Oxon OX14 4RN

and by Routledge
605 Third Avenue, New York, NY 10158

Routledge is an imprint of the Taylor & Francis Group, an informa business

© 2022 Grant Duncan

The right of Grant Duncan to be identified as author of this work has been asserted in accordance with sections 77 and 78 of the Copyright, Designs and Patents Act 1988.

All rights reserved. No part of this book may be reprinted or reproduced or utilised in any form or by any electronic, mechanical, or other means, now known or hereafter invented, including photocopying and recording, or in any information storage or retrieval system, without permission in writing from the publishers.

Trademark notice: Product or corporate names may be trademarks or registered trademarks, and are used only for identification and explanation without intent to infringe.

British Library Cataloguing-in-Publication Data
A catalogue record for this book is available from the British Library

Library of Congress Cataloging-in-Publication Data
A catalog record has been requested for this book

ISBN: 978-1-032-13462-8 (hbk)
ISBN: 978-1-032-13463-5 (pbk)
ISBN: 978-1-003-22930-8 (ebk)

DOI: 10.4324/9781003229308

Typeset in Bembo
by Apex CoVantage, LLC

To Sarah
My wife, my best friend, my navigator

CONTENTS

	Contributors	xi
	Acknowledgements	xiii
1	Introduction	1
2	The three ages of man	5
3	And the ages of woman?	11
4	Gen X, Y, Z . . . whatever	19
5	On entrepreneurs	25
6	The context for success	29
7	Looking in the mirror	43
8	Where the rubber hits the road	49
9	Defining your archetype	65
10	Get out more	71
11	Going social	79
12	The endgame game	85
13	Conclusion	91
14	Twelve journeys	93
	Index	111

CONTRIBUTORS

Alan Jope

Amanda Mackenzie, OBE

Brent Hoberman, CBE

Caroline Hudack

Carrie Timms

Cecile Frot-Coutaz

Craig Mullaney

Dame Cilla Snowball, DBE

Dame Jayne-Anne Gadhia, DBE

Edgar Berger

Eve Williams

Gavin Patterson

Guy Laurence

Jeremy Haines

John Smith

Jonathan Lewis

Julietta Dexter

June Felix

Karen Blackett, OBE

Liv Garfield, CBE

Maria Kyriacou

Melanie Smith, CBE

MT Rainey, OBE

Nicola Mendelsohn, Baroness Mendelsohn, CBE

Oliver Snoddy

Rita Clifton, CBE

Roger Davis

Sir Peter Bazalgette

Sophie Adelman

Sophie Turner Laing, OBE

Stephen A. Carter, Baron Carter of Barnes, CBE

Stevie Spring, CBE

Tamara Ingram, OBE

Tim Davie, CBE

Toby Horry

Tristia Harrison

Val Gooding, CBE

William Eccleshare

Winnie Awa

Zillah Byng Thorne

ACKNOWLEDGEMENTS

Apparently, everybody has a book in them. In my case, it wasn't a potboiler or bodice-ripper. Instead, it was a business book, conceived and written during the 'Great Pandemic' of 2020.

Despite being a business book, it's quite autobiographical. The contents are a reflection of 40 years of my life spent in business, working initially in advertising and then as a headhunter. Its 30,000 or so words synthesise much of what I've learnt during that time and for that I have to thank those people who had a profound influence on me.

For one, my father, born to a working-class family in the northeast of Scotland who, with a combination of natural intelligence, guile, charm, hard work, and at times, ruthlessness, escaped the narrow confines of a Scottish fishing village to become a successful international advertising executive, living and working in Asia, Latin America, and then London.

Somewhat to his disappointment, I also went into advertising but there learnt the art of adaptability and resilience, focusing on what really matters and how to get the best out of mercurial, brilliant people. From Nigel Clark, my boss at CDP, I learnt that you can be a respected leader as well as a nice guy, from Unilever executive Richard Rivers, how to think strategically, and from talented creative people like Robert Saville, Indra Sinha, and Tony Brignull, the art of sublime writing.

During my second career, I have learnt the science as well as the art of executive search in the gold standard cultures of Spencer Stuart and Korn Ferry.

In many ways, the synthesis of these two worlds can be seen in the list of contributors who have helped amplify the ideas and strategies set out in this book. Thank you for your time and your commitment to me.

Also a specific thank you to Patrick Insole for his witty and thought-provoking illustrations.

And last but not at all least, a heartfelt thank you to my contributor Rory Marsden. The son of my closest friends, Philip and Val Marsden, Rory (or Roo to his family and friends) worked alongside me for nearly six months researching and building on the core themes that the book explores.

INTRODUCTION

Let me start with a metaphor.

My first job was at an ad agency. I was a graduate trainee in what was, at the time, one of the most creative agencies in the world, Collett Dickenson & Pearce. (Puttnam, Powell, and Lowe, the British agency that acquired Sterling Cooper in Mad Men, was loosely based on CDP.)

An important part of your basic training was to work on an account that would teach you the ropes.

In my case, this was the Metropolitan Police's recruitment advertising account. The gruelling day-to-day job was processing hundreds of small tactical press ads. But the upside was gaining an insight into one of the most high-profile and challenging jobs in the UK, if not the world: policing London.

As part of my induction, I was seconded for 24 hours to a local police station. This turned out to be in Stoke Newington, now colonised by the young middle classes ("Stokeys"), but then, an edgy working-class part of London.

It was early evening. I was milling around the police station when a "shout" went up – police lingo for an emergency call. I was grabbed by the officer who'd been chaperoning me to join him and his colleagues in one of their Incident Response Vehicles (squad cars to you and me).

We swung out onto Stoke Newington High Street. It was now rush hour and the streets were gridlocked, but somehow the driver steered effortlessly through the traffic, overtaking cars and jumping lights at speed.

It turned out that the incident was nothing more than a drunken altercation at a kebab shop. But what really intrigued me was how this police car had travelled at times at nearly 60 miles an hour through the built-up, traffic-laden streets of north London without crashing.

I asked the driver afterwards how he did this. He explained that a critical part of the training was to educate your brain not to focus on the car in front but the car beyond that. In time, your brain quickly processes and allows for the car in front of you. The real processing is about anticipating the actions of the car beyond so that you can leap forward and gain valuable seconds in order to arrive at your destination as quickly as possible.

This image has stayed with me over the years and become a metaphor for life and, within that, one's career.

Time and time again I meet people whose careers have been defined by following the car in front; leaving university and starting in banking, for example, because of a family contact, and then never leaving that industry; joining a big organisation and being continuously promoted until they find, 20 years down the line, that they are a company lifer.

I became intrigued by people who had, like the police squad car driver, looked beyond the car in front to take advantage of opportunities to accelerate beyond the immediately visible.

*

This book captures 40 years working with, talking to, and assessing executives with many different career journeys. It tries to offer a toolkit to help those who are thinking they need a change. And, crucially, it will help you to avoid getting stuck following the car in front.

To take this beyond the theoretical, I have also had the privilege to interview a number of top executives whose careers have been defined by their decision to look beyond the car in front.

It is not a panacea. It's a collection of interconnected ideas and techniques that have helped many executives I have worked with to make sense of the journey they've been on and, critically, the journey ahead.

Much of it has emerged from my own personal experience too. I was as conservative as they come at the start of my career. I spent 25 years in advertising moving seamlessly from one job and one firm to the next. I became a managing director at the age of 35 and chief executive by the age of 40. I persuaded myself that this was the right strategy.

And then I reached my late 40s, woke up, and saw that I was going to run out of road in the next few years. I had no strategy, no plan, and no idea about what was going to happen next. For the first time, I moved out from behind the car in front. I took a big risk and was lucky enough (because it was luck) to land in the world of executive search which has proved to be a genuinely enjoyable and fulfilling career ever since.

The professional journey we all go on is typically a mixture of hard work, good luck, and brain power. To avoid, like me, having to rely a little too much on the luck part, it helps to have a strategy and to be proactive with your choices and decisions, because taking control of your career can increase your chances of being happier and more fulfilled, both in your work life and elsewhere. I want to give you the tools to be able to do that so that whether you're in the early stages of your career or well on your way down the road, you can make plans and decisions that work best for you.

This book and its supporting case histories are an acknowledgement that we all need to think ahead and then get ahead of the situations we find ourselves in and take more of an assertive, strategic stance on our career choices.

That way we will no longer be at the mercy of the car in front.

THE THREE AGES OF MAN

Believe it or not, we can get stuck following the car in front before we're even allowed a driving license. That's right; this starts early, because our attitudes towards our own potential begin to be shaped, inevitably, in childhood. And they can come to define us.

It is crucial from the outset then to understand when, where, how, and why we become stuck in traffic, only moving when others do, instead of taking active control of the steering wheel.

THE CURSE OF THE FIXED MINDSET

There has been much discussion in recent years about fixed versus growth mindsets. In her definitive book on the subject, Stanford psychology professor Carol Dweck defines the former as the belief "that your qualities are carved in stone [which] creates an urgency to prove yourself over and over." Those with growth mindsets, meanwhile, believe "the hand you're dealt is just the starting point for development [and] your basic qualities are things you can cultivate through your efforts, your strategies, and help from others."[1] She defined the two mindsets after carrying out research which involved setting a group of children progressively harder and harder puzzles to solve. Some reached the point where they felt that the puzzles were impossible, their intelligence was being judged, and they had been found wanting. But others viewed the harder puzzles as a challenge and relished the opportunity to learn. They hadn't failed; they just hadn't got it yet.

It is not difficult to see the link between the fixed mindset and following the car in front. If you don't believe you can learn new skills or successfully strike out into a new sector, there is a tendency to stick with what you know. It is the painful result of cycling too fast as a child and crashing into a bollard; the embarrassment of getting an answer wrong in the school classroom; and the humiliation of peer-group rejection. Like I said, this starts early.

This is not to say that, as you become an adult, you can't be the very best insurance broker around. But it could mean that you're not pushing the boundaries to become a mould-breaking disruptor of the insurance category despite the fact that you are super bright and super capable. The fixed mindset means staying in your lane, staying in your comfort zone.

Just about every one of the successful executives I interviewed while researching this book opted to make a change when the easier, more comfortable option would have been to stay put. Gavin Patterson, former BT plc CEO before becoming Chief Revenue Officer and President of Silicon Valley software giant Salesforce, started his career in the hotbed of talent that was Procter & Gamble in the 1990s. He spent nine years there before moving to Telewest in 2000. On this decision, Patterson says: "I had plenty of runway ahead of me at P&G, but I wasn't sure where it was going to take me."

Similarly, Clear Channel CEO William Eccleshare opted for a major change in late 1999, when he was CEO of advertising agency Ammirati Puris Lintas. Running APL was comfortable. He was surrounded by great people – many of whom he'd hired – and it was "a lot of fun." But he knew he was going nowhere. "I remember thinking from my career point of view: I need to get control again or something's going to happen that I'm not comfortable with." So he made a change, joining consultancy giants McKinsey in 2000, where he admits to feeling a cultural misfit. "It was no fun at all," he says. But it was a decision that got him to where he is today.

Tim Davie, Director-General of the BBC, started his career alongside Patterson at P&G in the early 1990s before joining PepsiCo as UK Marketing Manager in 1993. Twelve years later, he made the move to the BBC, but he says he could quite easily have stayed at Pepsi: "Financially I would have been a lot better off. But actually, it was better to jump out and go to a new sector by a mile."

These are all growth mindset decisions. Having a growth mindset – or "staying open minded" as Informa plc CEO Stephen Carter describes it to me – is key to gaining the tools to break out from behind the car in front. And it is eminently possible to change from a fixed to a growth mindset – tactics we'll discuss in later sections.

Unfortunately, though, it is not only a fixed mindset that prevents people from making progressive, beneficial career decisions.

MIDLIFE CAUTION (OR HOW TO RESPOND TO RESPONSIBILITY)

As a young professional, career progression will often come naturally, particularly if you have a growth mindset, and are motivated and bright. Risk-taking is a whole lot easier when you have only yourself to look after and your whole life ahead of you. You might not think twice, for example, about taking that posting abroad or joining an exciting if risky startup.

But something I see again and again is the caution that comes from increased responsibility, both professionally and personally.

Some people become the victims of their own success. Rising quickly through the ranks and getting promoted early can become a real disabler if you retrench into risk aversion in order to avoid making any mistakes that lose you the leadership role you worked so hard to achieve. At the same time, people get married, have children, and take on mortgages. And therein lies the other disabler: fear of losing everything you've worked for and fear of letting your family down. (This is exactly what happened to me in my mid-30s when I became the managing director of the ad agency Gold Greenlees Trott.)

These are completely legitimate concerns. And if you're on the right road, why wouldn't you follow the lead of the car in front? Because you won't be in control. Paradoxically, the cautious approach can often be the least responsible, as you're effectively kicking the can down the road. Tim Davie puts it this way: "In order to keep yourself happy in a career and make good career choices, you need to get more comfortable with more risk. More risk is the safer choice."

In other words, hunkering down is not the only way to respond to additional responsibility. There are other options which will pay greater dividends later on.

INTO THE CUL-DE-SAC

There will be people reading this book thinking, "Oh dear, I have been following the car in front and I am now sitting in a cul-de-sac."

In fact, I suspect the majority of executives have at some moment found themselves heading down a one-way street only to find that a dead end is looming. The truth is that if you hunker down, play it safe, keep following the car in front, then there will come a point when you will hit a dead end, often without seeing it coming. Typically, these are executives in their late-40s, early-50s. They have had a successful career (although perhaps not successful enough to give two fingers to working life). But the road on which they've been travelling has come to an end – a new chairman or CEO with new ideas, an economic downturn and a restructuring of expensive management, a merger where there's two of everything. Or simply getting up in the morning to go to work is simply not exciting. Everything feels like Groundhog Day.

The original intention of this book was to help executives with tools and techniques to stop them from ever turning into the cul-de-sac. But as I have talked to more people, I have realised that only the fortunate few have had the foresight or simply the good luck to overtake and accelerate towards a new destination. Truth be told, I am in many ways an example of someone who followed the car in front for far too long. I spent 25 years in advertising being promoted and headhunted all the time so, surely, this was the right course of action? But luckily I saw that dead end looming and made a decision to change course in the nick of time (I was nearly 50).

So my message to those of you who feel stuck is that you can reverse out of that cul-de-sac. It will need self-awareness and courage, the wherewithal (financially and emotionally) to "take a hit" as you traverse to something new. But several of the approaches in this book can help you get there.

In particular, I would point you to Chapter 8 – Where the Rubber Hits the Road. In *Three Questions, Competencies not Curriculum Vitae,* and *Exploring your Solar System*, you will find strategies for looking at yourself and your capabilities from a different angle, refreshing the way you think about and position yourself, and digging out skills and strengths that have got lost under layers of corporate sediment. Also take a look at Chapter 12, the Endgame Game. The title sounds rather final and, to a certain extent, it's about ending one career chapter and beginning another. But this doesn't have to be about "life after full-time employment." You can also use it to think about jumping onto a new ladder which may provide much more fulfilment than the one that you have spent the last 10, 20, or 30 years climbing.

So whether you are making good progress on your journey or are stuck in that cul-de-sac, the rest of this book should help you take control of getting you to the right destination.

NOTE

1 Dr Carol S. Dweck (2017). *Mindset: Changing the Way You Think to Fulfil Your Potential*. Robinson.

AND THE AGES OF WOMAN?

It is important to address the fact that, while the pathway outlined in *The Three Ages of Man* is a classic one, it is far from a universal route through an executive career. Not everyone is content with gradually progressing up the corporate ladder fairly comfortably into their late 40s/early 50s. More importantly, though, not everyone, even if they are incredibly talented and driven, is given that option.

In March 2020, *Business Leader* magazine ran an article headlined: "Discover the Female FTSE 100 CEOs of 2020."[1] The reason they needed "discovering" is that there were only five of them: Emma Walmsley (GlaxoSmithKline), Liv Garfield (Severn Trent), Carolyn McCall (ITV), Alison Brittain (Whitbread), and Alison Rose (Royal Bank of Scotland Group, as it then was). Fortunately, that's easy maths: it's 5%. That's only a single point increase from eight years before (2012), when there were four. At that rate, it will take more than 80 years before women achieve equality at the CEO level.

The Fortune 500 fares a little better. In May 2020, the record number of female CEOs included on the prestigious list was headline news, literally.[2] But it was still only a paltry 37. That's slightly harder maths, but not by much, and it comes out at 7.4%.

What I'm getting at is, despite being a good way into the third decade of the 21st century, it is still roughly 10 times as hard for women to get top executive jobs as men.

The purpose of the toolkit provided in this book is to help executives of any gender make better, more strategic career decisions. It is, however, quite clearly necessary to acknowledge that women face different challenges in lots of executive environments. It is impossible for me to provide adequate advice on how to deal with these.

DOI: 10.4324/9781003229308-3

So I have turned to some of the most successful female executives I know who have generously offered their best pieces of advice on how women can navigate an executive career.

BE YOURSELF

Perhaps the headline piece of advice, mentioned by just about every single one of the 15 top female executives I spoke to for this section, is to be yourself.

"It's a ridiculous cliché," says Tristia Harrison, CEO of TalkTalk, "but it's hard to be happy if you're pretending to be someone else or trying to fit a mould others have created for you. We interact and collaborate best when we have a social connection with colleagues, so don't be afraid to talk about your family, hobbies, or things that make you unique."

Liv Garfield, CEO of Severn Trent plc, has similar advice. "It's genuinely important to bring the real you to work every day and be open about what's going well at home and what's not," she says. "I believe previously this was seen as a sign of possible female weakness. Actually it's the opposite."

For Sophie Turner Laing, former CEO of Endemol Shine Group, this remains important throughout your career and is vital for female leaders: "Really be yourself. You want people to understand what makes you tick. You want to show people what your values are and what's important to you and how you're going to work with them to make a difference to their lives as well as the customers' lives."

Meanwhile, Global Chairman, Wunderman Thompson, Tamara Ingram advises: "Have a personal vision for what you want, and focus on that vision. Don't get tripped up by the day to day. Have clarity of focus on the vision."

In the same vein, Maria Kyriacou, President of ViacomCBS Networks International, Australia, Israel, and UK, and Karen Blackett, CEO of Group M, both stress the importance of using difference to your own benefit.

"You may well find that throughout your career you are often the only female voice in the room," says Blackett, "use the fact that you stand out to your advantage."

And Kyriacou advises: "At probably many points, you will be the odd one out. The 'other' that isn't part of the group. So you have to be honest about who you are, because it's too emotionally draining to pretend to be someone else."

Amanda Mackenzie, the Chief Executive of Business in the Community, provides a useful caveat; a recalibration if you will: "The phrase 'be yourself' isn't *always* helpful; finding a way to be comfortable with how you show up is worth aiming for. When do you do your best work? When are you least self-conscious to speak up? Where do you get your energy from? What do your colleagues and friends most value about you? Therein lie the ingredients for how to get comfortable and appreciative of what you bring."

Cecile Frot-Coutaz, Chief Executive of Sky Studios, adds: "Be comfortable doing it your own way. Have your own style. It's ok to lean into your own style."

ALWAYS BE LEARNING

Another common thread that emerged along with being yourself is the need to always keep learning.

Val Gooding, former CEO of Bupa, describes it as getting qualified for the career you aspire to. "Read widely," she says, "be knowledgeable about businesses, sectors, and the wider economy. Be aware of 'today's issue'."

On the actual practicalities of how to go about this, Nicola Mendelsohn, VP EMEA at Facebook, has her own strategy. "It's so important to keep learning," she says. "Something that works for me is 'vision writing.' I write down what I want to accomplish during the year ahead – my vision for the future. Research shows you're forty two per cent more likely to do something if you write it down and share it with people."

Liv Garfield is insistent on the need to "learn from as many people and experiences as possible." The best ideas, she says, often come from unexpected sources, so listen to everything people say.

Almost identical advice comes from Cilla Snowball, former group CEO of advertising giant AMV BBDO: "Keep learning and listening, and stay curious. You will develop faster with wider career and personal interests. Your reach should exceed your grasp."

The last point that your reach should exceed your grasp touches on the notion of ambition. The psychiatrist Anna Fels has previously written in the *Harvard Business Review* that the women she interviewed for an investigation into female ambition "hated the very word. For them, 'ambition' necessarily implied egotism, selfishness, self-aggrandizement, or the manipulative use of others for one's own ends. None of them would admit to being ambitious."[3] And it is notable that the word rarely occurred in my discussions for this section.

When it did with, for example, Amanda Mackenzie, it was just one of a number of factors she believes are essential to successfully managing a career: "Aim for a combination of ambition and delivery, team work, strength, and leadership."

Maybe it's just a difference in interpretation. Ambition, no. But purpose, aspiration, intent? A resounding yes. "Care a little bit more," says Tamara Ingram. "I've often wondered why people do get to the top versus others. And my conclusion is: the person who cares a little more, who does a little more, is into the detail a little bit more – who anticipates the needs of their team, their clients, their stakeholders – they will always succeed further, or go further, or reach their goals, because they're adding value faster than others."

FIND ALLIES, BUILD A SUPPORT NETWORK

That ambition is a potentially dirty word among women is perhaps an indication of a far greater capacity and inclination to work together. Ensuring you don't try to go it alone was another major theme of my conversations for this section.

"Go out of your way to make friends and allies among your colleagues," was another of Val Gooding's recommendations. "All too often, women are very focused on results, and don't pay enough attention to building long-term alliances."

It is essential, says Liv Garfield, for women to embrace early on in their careers that they will need help. This means both at work and at home. "We all need a strong support network, especially if you are a working mum," she says. Sophie Turner Laing puts it like this: "You don't have to do everything yourself."

For Karen Blackett, it's about finding your cheerleaders and your sponsors. "Every career journey will have its ups and downs," she says, "your cheerleaders know all of you – what you are truly capable of and just how far you could go, but also what your insecurities are."

"Keep them close, as they will help you celebrate every success (and you should take a moment to celebrate), as well as pick you up and help you keep going after each low. They will help you keep it real and keep it moving. As well as cheerleaders, every female executive needs a sponsor. Someone to advocate for her in the rooms she may not have access to as yet, to talk about what you are capable of and your talent. They have skin in the game to see you progress and succeed."

And it is crucial, according to Sophie Turner Laing, to be that support network, to be the mentor and sponsor yourself when you get to the position that it is possible: "Because there aren't many women role models – particularly in male-dominated industries – it's beholden to you to put your hand back down and pull the next generation up behind you."

Allied to that is the need to be a good example for the women below you. To set the trends. "If you are a leader, particularly a new leader, particularly a woman," says MT Rainey, "remember you loom much larger to others than they do to you, or indeed than you do to yourself. Be aware of the weight your words, actions, attitudes, and values carry."

One of the key pieces of advice given by Jayne-Anne Gadhia, former Virgin Money CEO and founder of money-saving app Snoop, gives is: don't sacrifice family for work.

Expanding further, she explains: "It can be particularly destructive to think that you're hooked to the way everybody else operates, even if you're executing your own role properly. I was certainly caught up in wanting to be the last person out the door when I was 'growing up' at work. But then I realised as an executive, as we started to talk about work-life balance, that you can only achieve that if, as a leader, you're prepared to do it. I remember at Virgin Money, in particular, consciously working to leave the office at six o'clock whatever happened and manage my life around that."

"There's a difficult thing to work through, as a woman in particular, which is: how can I be a brilliant leader and a boss and treat everybody equally and allow people also to live their own work-life balance if I don't live my own work-life balance? I actually think the most successful people are the ones who get that balance right."

THERE'S A TIME TO PRETEND

I initially titled this final section *Fake It*, and was so close to adding "till you make it" on the end that it's genuinely embarrassing. I was, though, spared from the fiery hells of hackneydom by the insight of Rita Clifton, former UK CEO and Chairman of Interbrand, who had this to say on that particularly tired phrase: "I'm a bit allergic to the 'fake it till you make it' type of advice; that can encourage people to think of themselves at work as some kind of third-party corporate construct, or inhuman avatar. And that kind of fake persona running businesses is exactly what's *not* needed if we're to help the world work better all round."

"I vividly remember when I first became CEO and tried to enact the kind of 'kick-ass CEO persona' that I thought was required by my corporate owners. It might well have been, but it definitely did not suit me or my real management style long term. 'Faking it' might suit a TV programme but you can't go on faking stuff day in, day out in your professional or personal life without making yourself miserable or ill."

I think she's absolutely right. And to preach about "faking it" not long after urging people to "be themselves" borders on the hypocritical.

But there are scenarios when to pretend, to fake, to act like you are full of confidence, when you actually feel like curling up in the corner in the foetal position, is not only the right way to go, but the only way if you're to make progress. And it's an idea that came up a lot in my discussions for this section.

Lack of confidence, self-doubt, and harsh personal scrutiny seem to be particularly prevalent traits in female executives. In order to get over these, it is not necessary to expunge them from your personality; you just have to put on a play.

Sophie Turner Laing is convinced that men have the same confidence issues as women do; she just thinks they're (that is to say, we're) better at covering them up. "Women have got to learn to be brave," she says. "I always use the analogy: it's like putting makeup on. You put this kind of armour plating on and you can be like total jelly on the inside, but never let anybody see that. We've all been off to cry in the loo at some stage in our careers: men and women!"

You don't need to be confident, merely to *appear* to be confident. The appearance of confidence is nearly as good as confidence itself. And one might lead to the other.

What is most important, though, is that you own your own working methods, in every scenario. If *you're* not confident, don't sit by and let other, potentially less-capable colleagues progress past you because *they* are. Identify ways you're going to remove your own blockers and put them into action.

Cilla Snowball encapsulates this idea with admirable pithiness. "Career progression," she says, "is about active responsibility not passive reward. About thoughtful, choiceful strategy on your part rather than placing yourself at the mercy of others, or luck, or fate."

★

It would be impossible for me to distil all the advice that was so generously passed on to me for this chapter without writing an entirely new book. I have tried, though, to relay the key themes that emerged as pithily and instructively as possible.

It is an unfortunate truth that there are additional challenges for women who are attempting to navigate a successful executive career. The advice outlined earlier will, with any luck, make it easier to overcome those.

NOTES

1 www.businessleader.co.uk/discover-the-female-ftse-100-ceos-of-2020/81145/
2 www.dailymail.co.uk/news/article-8333869/Record-number-37-women-CEOs-rank-years-Fortune-500-list.html
3 https://hbr.org/2004/04/do-women-lack-ambition

GEN X, Y, Z . . . WHATEVER

And then what of those who might have read the first chapter and thought the classic model for an executive career is antiquated? That the linear, climbing-the-ladder career is dead and buried, and nobody is even given the option of following the car in front anymore. To an extent, that is true. Careers are more volatile in the 21st century. And staying at one company, or even in one industry, for one's entire career is rarely possible any more.

But the widespread idea that different generations – specifically younger generations – want different things from work, or that they operate in noticeably different ways, is misleading. It's not so black and white. Believe it or not, millennials and baby boomers are not all that different. The priority, the ideal, remains the same: a linear career which provides the security of full-time employment. Or as a 2016 survey put it: "Like those in every generation before them, millennials strive for a life well-lived. They want good jobs – ones with 30-plus hours of work a week and regular paychecks from employers."[1]

SPANNING THE GENERATIONS

While aims and methods across the generations are more similar than you might think, it is true that the current work environment is different from what has come before it, because, for the first time in history,[2] five different generations are working side by side. As people continue to live and work longer, it certainly won't be the last time that happens.

Right now it is eminently possible that a single team at a company could include members of the Silent Generation (born pre-1945;

DOI: 10.4324/9781003229308-4

think Joe Biden, Nancy Pelosi), baby boomers (born 1946–1964; think Bill Gates, Oprah Winfrey), Gen X (1965–1980; Elon Musk, Reese Witherspoon), millennials (1981–1996; Mark Zuckerberg, Megan Rapinoe), and Gen Z (1997–2012; Malala Yousafzai, Greta Thunberg). Besides the entertainment value, there is in considering how a Biden/Oprah/Musk/Zuckerberg/Malala team might operate, there is greater value in understanding that people of such disparate ages operate together in the workforce every single day. And most importantly, the way they work and their ambitions are not all that different.

A major study into generational differences in the workplace conducted in 2012 opened: "There is a growing sense among a group of authors, consultants, trainers, and management gurus that there are substantive and meaningful generational differences between individuals in today's workplace."[3] But the study's authors concluded that this sense of differing methods and ambitions between the generations – which is so often a given in media representations of the workplace – is inaccurate.

A MARATHON NOT A SPRINT

So it's the work environment that has changed, not workers themselves. Millennials are often accused of being fickle job hoppers, but that is largely down to the fact that they are currently among the younger members of the workforce, and young people tend to change jobs often. Indeed, a 2017 study found that "millennial workers are just as likely to stick with their employers as their older counterparts in Generation X were when they were young adults."[4] The same is likely to be true again of Gen Z, who will be enticed by exactly the same thing that attracted their older counterparts when they were younger: a decent wage, job security, a good work environment, and the chance to progress.

But what is certainly true is that the average time a younger employee plans to spend at their current job is less than those above them. The velocity of change is much faster. A member of, say, the baby boomer generation may have typically thought about their careers in 10-year increments and viewed it as a steady climb up the greasy pole until they reach the top job. But younger Gen Xers and millennials are different. To start with, their rate of change is much faster.

A global Manpower Group study from 2016 found that two-thirds of millennials thought less than two years was the "right" amount of time to spend in a single role.[5] Caroline Hudack, CMO at Impala and a former executive at Facebook and Airbnb, believes there's merit in this attitude and that sometimes staying in the same role or company could be perceived negatively. "If I see someone who has been at a company for more than 4 years," she says, "I'd really be looking for that person to demonstrate how they've continued to learn and grow, as well as their ability to adapt to new company cultures."

Then there's how younger workers view their own careers as opposed to their older counterparts. The same Manpower Group study found that "the millennial mindset sees individual jobs as stepping stones to self-improvement, rather than a final destination. Millennials have redefined job security as career security – it's the journey not the job."[6]

One of the key reasons for this difference in mindset is longevity. They know they've got time on their hands. More than half of millennials expect to work past the age of 65, over a third past their 70th birthday, and 12% believe it is likely they will work until they die.[7] So a career is no longer a mad dash to the finish line, it's more of a meander in which taking time to try out different things and learn new skills – and maybe even taking some time off – is perfectly acceptable. But there's another significant reason for the difference in attitude between older and younger cohorts in the workforce: the global financial crisis.

GENERATION 2008

If there are genuine distinctions to be made between older and younger people in the workforce, the typical baby boomer/GenX/millennial demographics are not the most helpful. A better dividing line is 2008, because it makes a major difference where you were in your career in the latter stages of the 2000s.

Those who had only recently entered the job market, were graduating into it, or came into it while the aftershocks of the global financial crisis were still being felt have been put on a worse lifetime-earnings trajectory than those older than them,[8] who were able to establish themselves during much rosier times and were far more secure when the shit hit the fan.

Eve Williams, eBay UK's chief marketing officer, was four years out of Cambridge University when the crisis came but still recalls a sense of huge uncertainty for her contemporaries, who were not yet quite established enough for comfort. "All of a sudden, it didn't feel safe, it didn't feel quite as secure as it had done."

The legacy of the crash has remained for a whole swathe of the workforce. Indeed, Annie Lowrey, an economic policy writer for *The Atlantic*, paints a fairly stark picture for Generation 2008: "[They] entered the workforce during the worst downturn since the Great Depression. Saddled with debt, unable to accumulate wealth, and stuck in low-benefit, dead-end jobs, they never gained the financial security that their parents, grandparents, or even older siblings enjoyed."[9]

It is a wonder, then, that many of the younger sections of the workforce aren't all disillusioned mopes. And they aren't. Manpower's survey found that "millennials are surprisingly upbeat about their careers."[10] And I think the reason for that lies in the perhaps surprising idea that, despite many claims to the contrary, younger people have much the same focus as their forebears when it comes to their careers: to make steady, linear progress. They are aware that sideways, or even backwards, moves may be necessary, and they are pragmatic enough to cope with them. But the end goal remains the same.

★

So whether you're reading this book in your 30s, still relatively early in your career, and looking for a toolkit that will help you map out the next few stages. Or you're in your 50s, and trying to ensure you finish your career with a flourish. The danger of following the car in front remains the same. The risk of finding yourself in a cul-de-sac persists. Staying in control of your own career and being prepared for what might lie ahead is a necessity, and over the remaining chapters, you will learn how to do just that. First, a quick aside.

NOTES

1 www.gallup.com/workplace/236477/millennials-work-life.aspx
2 https://hbr.org/2014/09/managing-people-from-5-generations
3 David P. Costanza, Jessica M. Badger, Rebecca L. Fraser, Jamie B. Severt and Paul A. Gade (2012). Generational Differences in Work-Related

Attitudes: A Meta-Analysis. *Journal of Business and Psychology*, Vol. 27, No. 4, pp. 375–394.
4 www.pewresearch.org/fact-tank/2017/04/19/millennials-arent-job-hopping-any-faster-than-generation-x-did/
5 www.manpowergroup.com/wps/wcm/connect/660ebf65-144c-489e-975c-9f838294c237/MillennialsPaper1_2020Vision_lo.pdf?MOD=AJPERES
6 Ibid.
7 Ibid.
8 www.theatlantic.com/ideas/archive/2020/04/millennials-are-new-lost-generation/609832/
9 Ibid.
10 www.manpowergroup.com/wps/wcm/connect/660ebf65-144c-489e-975c-9f838294c237/MillennialsPaper1_2020Vision_lo.pdf?MOD=AJPERES

ON ENTREPRENEURS

"A verbal error made by and considered characteristic of former U.S. president George W. Bush." That's how Oxford Languages[1] defines "Bushism." So numerous were the verbal gaffes of Dubya – who could forget, "They misunderestimated me," or the stunningly philosophical, "Rarely is the question asked: Is our children learning?" – that they coined a word for them.

Perhaps one of the best-remembered Bushims was his proclamation that "the trouble with the French is that they don't have a word for entrepreneur." The truth is that it's highly unlikely he ever actually said it. There's certainly no proof. Such a shame, really, as it's a Bushism par excellence.

Of course, entrepreneur *is* a French word – in the same way that cliche, boutique, souvenir, and genre are French words that we use all the time in English. Entrepreneur derives from the French word "entreprendre," which means "to undertake." To be clear, we're not talking about pissing other drivers off on the motorway by whizzing up the inside, nor are we organising a funeral, or watching WWE. We're talking about committing to do something. That type of undertaking.

And it's a revealing derivation. Because being an entrepreneur is, indeed, quite the undertaking. "It's not always a high," explains Winnie Awa, founder of Carra, with no little understatement. For Brent Hoberman, co-founder of Lastminute.com and Founders Factory, entrepreneurship is about "constantly overcoming obstacles and just a lot of experimentation; a lot of the new."

THE ADVENTURE ROUTE

Being an entrepreneur is very different to being a "normal" executive, such as there is one. It's a completely different path. Indeed, the lack of a pathway is an intrinsic part of the entrepreneur's journey.

Esteemed television entrepreneur Sir Peter Bazalgette frames his own career as one that is in diametric opposition to the car-in-front route. It started out fairly traditionally in 1977 when he joined the BBC as a news trainee after graduating from Cambridge. But more than four decades later, in contrast to some of his cohort who never left the BBC ("and had jolly good careers as journalists as predicted"), Bazalgette has ploughed his own, remarkably successful, furrow. Among his numerous credits, he is responsible for creating 1990s television stalwarts *Ready, Steady, Cook*, *Changing Rooms*, and *Ground Force* and bringing *Big Brother* to the UK. More recently, he was chair of Arts Council England from 2013 to 2016, after which he was appointed chairman of ITV. He picked up his knighthood in 2012.

Bazalgette is at pains to point out, though, that none of this was ever planned. "I just seized opportunities," he says. "And it seems to me that people who do have a career plan – and good for them – are taking fewer risks. An entrepreneur is a person inclined to take a few more risks. But there's no real plan. Just two principles. The first is carpe diem: seizing things as they arise because they seem interesting. And the other is zagging when other's zig."

Bazalgette speculates that there could be a genetic aspect to who's cut out for being an entrepreneur, pointing to the so-called "warrior gene" (MAOA-L, a variant of the MAOA gene that breaks down serotonin). MAOA-L has previously been linked to aggression and impulsivity, but carriers have also been found to be better at making risky decisions.[2] And Bazalgette believes it could be linked to a spirit of adventure, a key component to being an entrepreneur.

He summarises the attitude needed for being an entrepreneur: "Are you prepared to stick your neck out, take a few risks, be uncertain, not quite know what the outcome will be? Because you don't always know what the outcome will be."

"But somehow, if you move the pieces around on the chessboard, unexpected things happen. It's true that what might happen might be bad. But it also might be good. And since you're not entirely a victim of circumstance, you can guide; you can make decisions as you go along, and you can seize this opportunity or make that decision."

"It's not as though you're simply saying, 'I'm doing this and then I've got to put my hands in the air and see if it's good or bad.' Because you can make things good or bad. You can influence. You can make something of it."

GET A HAT RACK

When you're an entrepreneur, you don't have a manager, a corporate structure, a salary, a pension, and holidays. But you do have to be all things to all people; and wear every hat there is, even if it doesn't fit. Awa, who worked at Ernst & Young, Net-A-Porter, and ASOS before striking out on her own, explains the challenge of having to, for example, be her own recruiter: "When I was trying to hire a community and marketing lead, I'd never done that before."

"When I was at Asos and Net, the kind of people that I was hiring, they were people in the same field as me; in programme management, strategy, product management, digital product development. That's very, very different to hiring a marketing executive."

The eminent American economist Edward Lazear – who, incidentally, served as President Bush's chief economic advisor from 2006 to 2009 – theorised in a 2005 Stanford University study that "entrepreneurs must be jacks-of-all-trades who need not excel in any one skill but are competent in many."[3] He was clearly on to something. As well as wearing lots of different hats, entrepreneurship is about being fearless.

"Just go for it" is the advice of Julietta Dexter, founder of The Communications Store, now co-founder and chief growth and purpose officer at ScienceMagic.Inc. "It could be a failure but trying is what matters in the end. What if I fail? Will nobody like me? That quite simply does not matter."

"I think that's the humility that you do need as an entrepreneur because you've got to realise that sometimes the client's going to fire you. And it's you. It can be very personal when it's your own business. And then you've got to pick yourself up and dust yourself off, and there's nothing to rely on apart from yourself."

★

There are many lessons executives can learn from entrepreneurs – persistence, risk-taking, humility, and adaptability – because when you're an entrepreneur, there's no possibility of following the car in front; there isn't one. There's barely even a road; certainly not a well-trodden one.

Adding a dash of that coveted entrepreneurial spirit – that robustness, being active rather than passive, making change rather than letting it happen to you – is an excellent way to approach your career.

However, it is less easy for me to claim that all of the advice in this book, which focuses largely on executive careers, will be relevant for any entrepreneurs reading. Certainly, there will be useful sections, not least when we look at failure, an experience entrepreneurs have to deal with more often than most. But, on the other hand, the concept of grandmothers and egg sucking comes to mind when I think about instructing entrepreneurs on the benefits of risk-taking.

I mentioned earlier that the entrepreneur is to the car-in-front executive what Richard Dawkins is to the Pope, which is to say they're at different ends of the spectrum. The aim of this book, though, is not to make atheists of the devout, but to introduce at least a little agnosticism. So if you're keeping up, what I'm not saying is that any entrepreneurs reading this book should immediately throw it in the bin. But I am saying that this is not a book written specifically for entrepreneurs, so keep that in mind.

NOTES

1 www.lexico.com/definition/bushism
2 www.newscientist.com/article/dn19830-people-with-warrior-gene-better-at-risky-decisions/
3 Edward P. Lazear (2005). Entrepreneurship. *Journal of Labor Economics*, Vol. 23, No. 4, pp. 649–680.

THE CONTEXT FOR SUCCESS

For Gavin Patterson, a key tenet of successful career progress is to "never find yourself in a situation where you haven't got multiple ways out." To put it another way: try to avoid the cul-de-sac. The obvious solution is never to take the road to nowhere to begin with. But, failing that, the next best thing is to ensure you have the nous to find your way out.

Before we can talk about practicalities, we need to discuss attitude. To get out from behind the car in front, it is essential to have the right frame of mind. Only then is it possible to embrace the growth mindset, avoid the potential quagmire of early-midlife, and ensure you have the right directions to hand.

THE EARLY YEARS – TAKING A RISK

Spoiler alert, the title of this section is a bit of a clue to where I stand on risk-taking in career choices. But before dealing with that, it's worth talking about the first job.

The best way to characterise this is to use another metaphor (not mine but I love it). When a plane takes off, counterintuitively it heads into the wind. For the first 5–15 minutes, its only goal is to gain altitude, to trim its wings to be more efficient, and go further, in short, to fly. The distance covered in that time is often in the wrong direction or not particularly far. It doesn't matter in the scheme of things. It is merely a way to achieve "wheels up" faster.

This is a great way to think about a first job. A lot of people think they have to pick very carefully to ensure it is leading them in the right direction. In reality, it's more important to simply get airborne.

What happens after that is more complicated. Most ambitious people think about building their careers. But many, in particular the pre-millennial generations, tend to believe the best way to do so is through a series of progressive steps – climbing the rungs of the corporate ladder.

From what I've seen, this is not the best strategy. The most effective executives I have met have rarely advanced along such a linear path, or plotted out their route to the top, even when it might look like it.

Portfolio executive Stevie Spring, currently chairman of the British Council and Mind, says of her own career path that looking back on it through the rearview mirror, it looks very sensible. "But if you are looking at it from any point in the journey, it's a lot less clear." Similarly, Jonathan Lewis, CEO of outsourcing giants Capita plc, is keen to point out that, despite first appearances, his "wasn't some utopian career path."

Even Alan Jope, a career-long Unilever executive and now their CEO, says that "climbing the ladder absolutely was never an objective." The career strategy that has taken him to the top of Unilever was instead based on life experience.

"I can point to a pattern of being incredibly choosy on *where* I worked," he says, "and lacking any discrimination whatsoever on *what* the job was. In the belief that, actually, when you're on your deathbed, the thought 'Granny and I lived in Thailand for four years' is more likely to be a significant thing than 'I was brand manager of Sunsilk rather than Omo'."

Edgar Berger, now CEO of online car marketplace AutoScout24, made a fairly drastic early-career switch from management consultancy to television journalism and lived to tell the tale. "I was trading a well paid consultancy job that I had studied for," he says, "for an unpaid internship at a local TV station in Berlin. I felt like I was throwing away my whole career; I wanted to do it my way. And back in the day it felt like a huge decision, it felt pretty radical. But I don't think it was actually such a huge decision."

So the only real constant with the most successful executives is a breadth of experiences. And indeed the majority of employers, especially now, actively look for hires with that kind of diversity on their CV.

In the world of executive search, this is often termed a "mosaic career" and is much sought after for a number of reasons.

At the top of the list is simply the proven ability to operate outside your comfort zone which comes at a premium because the world is changing at such a rate that leaders are having to course-adjust on a daily basis.

So at a fundamental level, it speaks to an individual who has a track record of adaptability and delivery. It does take a particular skill to move seamlessly and successfully from one sector to another or from one role to another. No matter how able you are, you will be confronted with a whole set of differences around sector norms, culture, ways of working, functional requirements – often all at once. If you can survive those first critical years, then you have shown the requisite level of resilience and agility. Beyond that, you will also have delivered results which underline that you have mastered and had an impact on this new business.

The next benefit accruing from the mosaic career is the diversity of experiences you will gain. These could be geographical, functional (marketing, finance, operations, sales, technology), or scale of leadership (team size or complexion). In other words, a far wider range than you might get if you had stayed in your lane becoming a more senior, bigger marketer or finance director or head of sales. One of the benefits of working in a multinational is that these kinds of diverse experiences are baked into your management development. Alan Jope's career is a very good example of this – companies like Unilever have a huge range of different opportunities for executives who are willing to take on the challenge and the risk. But not all of us work in a multinational, so then it's about taking the risk of moving into genuinely uncharted territory.

These become the proof points that attract employers to people with these kinds of profiles – comfort operating outside your comfort zone and critically, succeeding.

As we will go on to talk about, this does not come without risk. Leaving the security of a world where you are a known entity and where you have built significant equity can be stressful. And sometimes, as we will see in some of the career journeys of the leaders who have contributed to this book, you can take a wrong turn. In my view, "mistakes maketh the man" and indeed, many employers I have worked with like career mistakes because of the battle scars and learnings that these executives will take from their experiences.

That all being said, a change of direction, in my estimation, is a risk worth taking in the context of the larger vision of one's career.

Having the courage to be open to trying out something new marks you out as brave and adaptable. The new experiences you gain can only amplify your strengths and build new capabilities.

UNBLOCKING THE BLOCKERS

A key factor in risk-taking is the more profound issue of your personality type. Taking a risk means being open to the fact there could be negative consequences, anything from physical injury to social rejection to financial losses. In academic studies, high risk-takers score high on three personality traits: impulsive sensation-seeking, aggression-hostility, and sociability.[1]

Genetics plays a role in risk-taking behaviour also. Identical twins separated at birth, for example, tend to engage in risk-taking behaviours at high rates. Testosterone appears to play a role as well, although the common conception that men are more prone to taking risks than women has been challenged recently.

Exeter University professor Michelle Ryan, for example, notes:

> Understanding the nature of gender differences in risk-taking is particularly important as the assumption that women are risk averse is often used to justify ongoing gender inequality – such as the gender pay gap and women's under-representation in politics and leadership.[2]

A team of psychologists, including Professor Ryan, established in a 2017 study that "women can be just as risky as men – or even riskier – when the conventional macho measures of daring – such as betting vast sums on a football game – are replaced by less stereotypical criteria."[3] Our whole attitude to risk, and what constitutes risky behaviour, is inherently gendered, and the study concluded that "when this bias is addressed, women and men rate themselves as equally likely to take risks."[4]

Taking risks eliminates the chance of looking back and asking: "what if?" It's also never too late to start taking risks. My own personal journey is testimony to this. After 25 years in advertising, I was bored and unfulfilled. I took the first big risk of my life which was to pack it all in with no job to go to. I then spent a year experimenting with lots of different options, industries, and ideas. It was during this journey that I discovered executive search, which opened a new fulfilling and productive chapter of my career.

I'm not saying you need to put your life and livelihood on the line every working day. Taking a risk can just mean doing something outside the norm, trying to get something done in an atypical way. Entrepreneur Winnie Awa, founder of personalised haircare platform Carra, has a nice take on doing things a bit differently.

"I always find a way to make things happen," she says. "I like to do things that seem like they're not possible to do. Even if it seems crazy. Even if it's messaging a celebrity to be on my board. I will do it, because why not? I messaged Rihanna by DM to ask her to be on my board! I do things like that because I believe that you've just got to try things. You just never know what could come out of it. She hasn't replied, but you never know."

Even if you take a risk that doesn't fully pay off – or doesn't pay off at all – you'll have gained more experience, more knowledge, which can help you to succeed elsewhere. There are studies that show that taking risks leads people to be more satisfied with their lives.[5]

Stephen Carter has had possibly the most diverse career of all the people I spoke to for this book. As a self-described "career entrepreneur," he has flitted between the public and the private sector – from commercial CEO/MD/COO at JWT(WPP plc)/NTL to founding CEO of the UK communications regulator, Ofcom, to chief of strategy for UK Prime Minister Gordon Brown to now, and for nearly the last decade, Group CEO at Informa plc.

While he observes that he wouldn't necessarily recommend his career choices to many people, he acknowledges that the variety of his experience – "all the risks that have gone with it, all the doubts that have gone with it, and all of the learning that has come with it" – is a large part of what has made him, hopefully, a better leader.

Because "the learning is a bit more seared into you than if you just steadily progress in the same role or the same company for 30–35 years through a machine process."

You gain more from taking risks than you do from not.

FAILING BETTER

As I touched on earlier, though, it is an aversion to risk that often bogs people down in the middle of their careers. The reason people are averse to risk is obvious: because with risk there is a possibility of failure. At the extreme end, an acute fear of failure (or atychiphobia, if you want to get fancy about it) can lead to a paralysing inability to even attempt anything that is not a sure thing. But it is the gentler, less immediately concerning side of atychiphobia that is one of the key reasons so many people end up following the car in front. A (perfectly understandable) inclination to play the percentages can often stop us from taking the risks that will lead to the bigger rewards, by which I do not exclusively mean financial rewards but also other, often more important benefits like job satisfaction, fulfilling your potential, making a difference, etc.

For many of us, this is the equation: risk ≈ failure. Risk could equal failure. And we don't want to fail. So how do you overcome that inherent fear of failure? You change the equation. Stop looking (exclusively) at the downsides of risk-taking, because while risk can equal failure, it can also, obviously, equal success. And if it doesn't end up equalling success, there are numerous other potential upsides to trying and failing than not trying at all, for example, the opportunity to learn, or to discover something new, or to meet new people.

Tchiki Davis, PhD, psychologist, author, and founder of The Berkeley Well-Being Institute, has presented a useful exercise in looking at failure. In short, she advises[6]:

1) **Find the benefits of past failures.** This will help you to understand that all negative experiences have some benefits and should make it easier next time you fail to understand those benefits in the moment rather than years later.
2) **When failure is possible, view it as a challenge.** This will help you to use the stress that comes with completing important tasks — tasks that you could fail at — to your advantage, rather than letting it paralyse you.
3) **Treat yourself kindly when you experience failure.** It is impossible to be perfect all the time. So don't try to be. If you fail, don't beat yourself up about it. Be kind to yourself and cultivate an attitude that can stave off guilt, shame, and embarrassment.

For Elizabeth Day, novelist, journalist, and host of the *How To Fail* podcast, "learning how to fail in life actually means learning how to succeed better."[7]

To offer a crude analogy, if you train to run a marathon but fall short of completing it, you are still better off because you are fitter than you were before. If you try again, you have a better chance of succeeding. It is the same in other aspects of life. Taking a risk, even if you fail, will help you develop emotional, intellectual, commercial fitness and help you build an essential resilience.

The truth is that there are times when you need to be resilient. When you hit a snake instead of a ladder, it is important to be able to take the positives from the experience, dust yourself down, and start moving up the board again.

Bupa chairman Roger Davis frames it like this: "I know some very successful people. I don't know any of them who've got there without a few setbacks along the way. And the thing that then determines who ends up at the top of the tree and who doesn't? Resilience. I do know people, good people, who had a setback and just haven't really been able to pick themselves up and get over it. So resilience is critical."

And for the moments when you've spent all the reserves of resilience you have? "You can bring in people to shore up your resilience when you need to," says Melanie Smith, CEO of Ocado Retail. "I've worked that out as I've got older; I'm better at asking for help."

Much of our attitude towards failure stems, again, from our mindset. To return to Carol Dweck, she uses the example of Billy Beane, of Moneyball fame. Before his pioneering use of sabermetrics helped him steer the under-funded Oakland Athletics to 20 consecutive wins and changed baseball forever, he was a sports sensation on the field, not off it.

When he was just a sophomore in high school, he was already the star of the basketball, football, and baseball teams. He was a natural, the next Babe Ruth, and as a result was a first-round pick in the 1980 MLB draft for the New York Mets. Despite all the talent in the world, though, he ended up a busted flush. As far as Dweck is concerned, it was because his fixed mindset meant he had a crippling fear of failure. "The minute things went wrong, Beane searched for something to break,"[8] she writes. Or as Michael Lewis put it in his book *Moneyball*: "It wasn't merely that he didn't like to fail; it was as if he didn't know how to fail."[9]

Knowing how to fail, and being okay with failure, is absolutely crucial to getting out from behind the car in front. In the oft-quoted words of Samuel Beckett: "Ever tried. Ever failed. No matter. Try again. Fail again. Fail better."[10]

This is not revolutionary thinking. It's Nike telling you to "Just Do It." It's Wayne Gretzky's "you miss 100 percent of the shots you don't take" attitude. It's just about every inspirational quote you've seen on a coffee mug or t-shirt. But if the attitude itself is easy to mine for a soundbite or slogan, the actual process of putting it into action is much harder. There are tools you need. And in the remainder of this book, I will give them to you.

★

One of the key things to remember is that a successful executive career does not happen in a vacuum. No matter what your ambitions, you will have to work effectively alongside others to fulfil them. The relationships you form throughout your career will have a major bearing on your success, because healthy work relationships are key to having a healthy career. (Interestingly, a 2018 poll found that people who have a best friend at work are seven times more likely to be engaged in their jobs.[11])

When you're starting out and you're at the bottom of the pile, the crucial thing is to simply try to create and maintain positive relationships with your co-workers and managers. And when you then take on leadership roles, your responsibility is in ensuring those below you can do that too. Obviously, though, all that is easier said than done. So let's take a look at some of the major barriers to forging effective relationships and how to overcome them.

IN THE FIRING LINE

Office politics are a fact of life in any organisation, big or small. They emerge from all kinds of things. Power struggles between individuals or groups, resentment (made worse if success was achieved through luck or subterfuge), overweening ambition, the sabotaging of your best efforts, and the list goes on. In today's more transparent world, it has become, thankfully, more acceptable to call out bad behaviour. But politics will always be there.

Especially if you're not comfortable with confrontation (which in my experience is the majority of people), politics can be tricky to handle. It's very easy to be crushed by them or to become a passive-aggressive contributor or simply to expend enormous amounts of energy trying to work around them. I say this because this is something I really struggled with. My instinct has always been to try to do the right thing. But I have often found myself outmanoeuvred and stressed by political machinations.

My first general management role was at an ad agency, a high-octane creative hot shop with a reputation for politics. In truth, I was so keen to get the title "Managing Director" that I ignored the warning signals. Within 12 months, I was in shreds, struggling with cultural organ rejection and ready to pack in my advertising career. In the event, I pushed on through. But I learned a huge amount about what proactive strategies worked for me.

So what can *you* do? How can you handle office politics and effectively manage conflicts that will inevitably emerge regularly throughout your career?

It's never easy, but at its heart, it's about being the bigger person, hitting the problem early, and elevating the situation by putting in place a framework that is rational rather than emotional. Here's a few crucial must-dos to ensure you deal with any office politics efficiently and effectively:

1) **Get in there early** – don't ignore conflicts. Identify them and deal with them early, because they won't just go away.
2) **Create an open environment** – ensure that everyone feels comfortable talking about difficulties in the open. As a manager, you need to be approachable in all situations.
3) **Manage difference positively** – guard against any "us and them" scenarios by creating a positive culture towards difference; whether it is difference in opinion, attitude, or lifestyle.
4) **Train in mediation** – oftentimes conflict resolution needs to be a more formal process. If you train as a mediator, you will be at the heart of resolving the issue.
5) **Genuinely engage with problems** – people just want to be listened to, so do that. Actively listen to issues and engage with them properly. And encourage others to do the same.
6) **Focus on causes not people** – personality differences and power inequities are so often the causes of office politics. So focus on resolving what is prompting conflicts to arise and try to avoid criticising those involved.
7) **Stay calm** – perhaps the most important piece of advice I can offer. Take that deep breath, remove emotion from conflicts,

and stay in control. Putting out a calm persona and leading by example is the best way to promote a positive environment.

ASKING "STUPID" QUESTIONS

In his 1995 book *The Demon-Haunted World*, the celebrated American astronomer Carl Sagan wrote: "There are naive questions, tedious questions, ill-phrased questions, questions put after inadequate self-criticism. But every question is a cry to understand the world. There is no such thing as a dumb question."[12]

To become successful – and, more significantly, to be exceptional – in your career, this is key advice to keep in mind. All too regularly even smart, hard-working people hamstring themselves by thinking that asking for clarification, asking questions, is a weakness or is in some way awkward or inconvenient. This can become amplified the higher up an organisation you go, when there is an expectation that, as a leader, you surely know the answer to everything. And it is an important disabler to tackle as early as possible to avoid it becoming embedded as a fear of failure. But the message is very simple: it's okay to ask questions. Even if you think the question stupid, ask it, because more often than not, it won't be stupid at all.

We've all been there. (This is important to remember, everyone really *has* been there, even the most capable, competent, intelligent people you know.) You're sitting in a meeting and colleagues are confidently throwing concepts or reference points around and you're thinking, "I've no idea what they're talking about." You don't want to be the one that puts up your hand to ask for clarification. But in truth, it's more than likely the majority of people in that meeting are also clueless – it's just that nobody wants to be *that* person.

Here's the skinny, though: you should want to be that person, because there aren't enough of that person. And being that person will make you exceptional. Just by the simple act of asking questions, you mark yourself out. A 2018 *Harvard Business Review* piece put it succinctly: most executives "don't ask enough questions, or pose inquiries in an optimal way. [And] few executives think of questioning as a skill that can be honed."[13] That is in contrast to, say, lawyers, journalists, or doctors, who are taught how to ask questions as an essential part of their training, and then consistently strive to ask better, more searching, questions throughout their careers.[14]

Over the years, I've come to see many examples where asking the "stupid" question not only gets an answer but also turns the individual who asks it into the smartest person in the room. (The past master at this was shambling detective Lieutenant Columbo. The baddy always underestimated his chaotic manner until, just as he was leaving the room, he would famously ask, "Just one more thing," teeing up an inescapable question which banged the criminal to rights.) A good question can do many things. As well as helping you learn, it also breeds confidence and insight. And perhaps most significantly, especially if you are in a senior position, it can promote genuine collaboration. If you can cultivate an environment in which everyone is confident enough to ask questions, you're onto a winner.

The best management consulting firms, like McKinsey, have built fantastically successful businesses simply by asking great questions. And this is the secret. There are ways of asking questions which, when crafted in the right way, expose sophistry and BS and, more importantly, uncover a rich vein of insights and understanding and turn you into the cleverest, not the stupidest, person in the room.

First things first then; if you're currently the type of person who stays quiet and is afraid of asking questions, just start asking them. Ask them often, ask them early, and ask them to anyone who will be able to help you out. And always be as specific as you can to ensure you're getting the answer you're looking for. Asking a vague, nebulous question in an attempt to sound smart while also getting the answer you need by stealth rarely works. It can also prompt rambling, time-consuming, and unhelpful answers. It can often help, especially for the more nerve jangling of situations, to scribble down a few versions of your question before deciding on the best one.

Now, if you think you're already inquisitive enough and don't have problems asking questions when you need an answer, the next step is to work out how you can ask even better questions, that will give you even better insights, and help you form even better relationships throughout your career. Here's a few key pointers to keep in mind:

1) **Listen properly** – it sounds so simple, but it's absolutely essential. If you've listened intently, you will avoid asking a question that has already been answered. You will also be able to ask questions that are genuinely insightful. Pre-preparing questions

is perfectly fine, but ensure that, when you ask them, they are relevant to the discussion taking place. Listening properly is the only way to guarantee this.

2) **Keep questions short** – try to limit your questions to a single sentence, without caveats or asides. It helps everyone involved keep focused. If you have a tendency towards verbosity or babbling, heed the advice mentioned previously and write questions down before you ask them.

3) **Don't ask statements** – a genuine plague of questioners worldwide. Any form of, "this is what you said, isn't it?" or "that's the point you were making, right?," is not really a question. It's a statement. And you're assuming an answer or at the very least trying to get the one you want. Ensuring your questions start with the word who, what, when, where, how, or why is a good way to avoid this.

4) **Follow-up** – there are two points here. The first is, if you're asking a question because you're unsure of something and you don't get the answer you need, don't give up. Ask again. The second is, asking follow-ups and picking up on points in a previous answer is the only way to create proper dialogues, which are at the core of business relationships.

5) **Keep asking questions** – practice makes perfect. And when it comes to asking questions, it's a virtuous circle. By asking questions, we naturally improve our emotional intelligence, which in turn makes us better questioners.

So that's how you ask questions of others, that is, how you get the most out of communication with colleagues and clients but what about asking questions of yourself?

NOTES

1 Marvin Zukckerman and D. Michael Kuhlman (2000). Personality and Risk Taking: Common Bisocial Factors. *Journal of Personality*, Vol. 68, pp. 999–1029.
2 www.exeter.ac.uk/news/featurednews/title_612350_en.html
3 Ibid.
4 Ibid.
5 www.webmd.com/balance/news/20050919/are-risk-takers-happier
6 www.psychologytoday.com/gb/blog/click-here-happiness/201804/three-ways-overcome-fear-failure

7 https://podcasts.apple.com/gb/podcast/s1-ep1-how-to-fail-phoebe-waller-bridge/id1407451189?i=1000415790730
8 Dr Carol S. Dweck (2017). *Mindset: Changing the Way You Think to Fulfil Your Potential*. Robinson.
9 Michael Lewis (2003). *Moneyball: The Art of Winning an Unfair Game*. Norton.
10 https://genius.com/Samuel-beckett-worstward-ho-annotated
11 www.gallup.com/workplace/236213/why-need-best-friends-work.aspx
12 Carl Sagan (2016). *The Demon-Haunted World: Science as a Candle in the Dark*. Random House.
13 https://hbr.org/2018/05/the-surprising-power-of-questions
14 Ibid.

LOOKING IN THE MIRROR

Between 1983 and 2013, a comic-strip called Le Chat, created by Belgian humourist Philippe Geluck, ran in the Belgian daily newspaper *Le Soir*. The eponymous hero was an anthropomorphic, regularly besuited cat who would stare out from his panels, expressionless but often looking directly at the reader, delivering absurd aphorisms and monologues. One of them went like this: "La mort, c'est un peu comme la connerie. Le mort, lui, il ne sait pas qu'il est mort. Ce sont les autres qui sont tristes. Le con, c'est pareil."[1]

Roughly translated, it means: "Death is a bit like stupidity. When you are dead, you do not know you are dead. It's only painful and difficult for others. It's the same when you are stupid."

Now, if you're nodding knowingly at that and muttering to yourself, "so true," wait right there! How do you know you're not the stupid one? Because you wouldn't, would you? Nor would I. It is this kind of brutal hilarity that made Le Chat (and Geluck) so popular. It's not just amusing worldpay; it's bang on. And it chimes with a crucial truism: we are pretty bloody awful at correctly estimating our own abilities.

THE DUNNING–KRUGER EFFECT

That's the conclusion Justin Kruger and David Dunning came to in their landmark 1999 study "Unskilled and Unaware of It."[2] Further than that, though, they found that the more unskilled you are, the more likely you are to overestimate your abilities. In other words, the less you know, the more you think you know. They also found the converse to be true: the greater your competency, the greater your

DOI: 10.4324/9781003229308-7

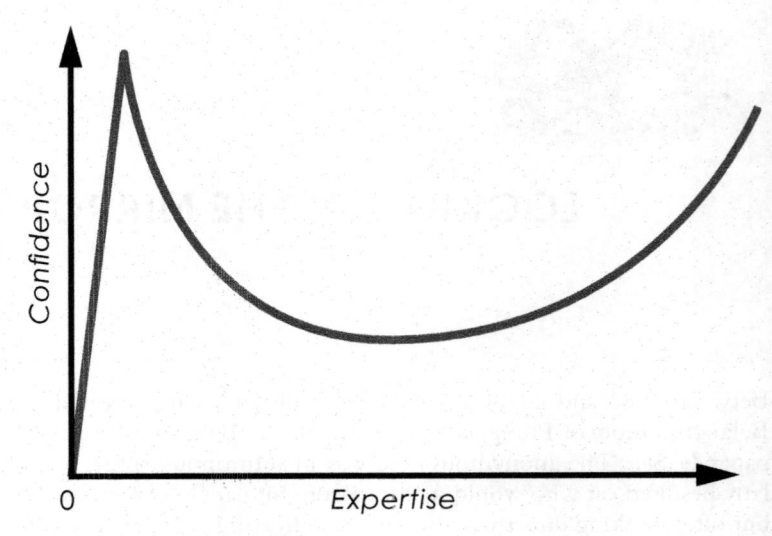

Figure 7.1 The Dunning–Kruger effect

awareness of your own limitations. Or as President John F. Kennedy put it in his "We choose to go to the Moon" speech in 1962: "The greater our knowledge increases, the greater our ignorance unfolds."

So why do I bring this up here? Well because self-awareness is absolutely vital to ensure you're going about your career in the right way. And the best and quickest way of establishing what your strengths and, perhaps more importantly, your weaknesses are is to ask other people. That means actively seeking out feedback. Relying only on self-appraisal is a threat to your own progress.

DON'T GET TOO COMFORTABLE

"Ignorance is bliss,"[3] the English poet Thomas Gray wrote in 1742. For many, that is their attitude to feedback, and understandably so, because receiving feedback is hard, especially if it's negative. And no matter who you are or how good you are, there is always going to be some negative feedback. That is why many people will only take feedback when it's thrust upon them. Otherwise, if they're doing just fine, getting the occasional slap on the back, and not getting on anyone's bad side, they're happy to just chug along (often behind the car in front).

That is why actively and regularly seeking out feedback, and being open to it is so important, because it gives you insight other people don't get. It puts you above the mean. Seeking feedback is an acknowledgement that you might be falling short, that you might, in fact, be average, even if it's only in one small area of what you do. Paradoxically, that acknowledgement is a sure-fire way to become above average.

That is not to say that to excel you need a crippling dose of impostor syndrome. But a healthy amount of self-doubt is far from a bad thing because it prevents you from getting too comfortable. That, in turn, ensures you are always doing not just a good job, but a better job than those around you, those who are happy they're doing just fine. So how do you go about getting the kind of feedback that is going to give you an edge?

LOOK AT YOURSELF FROM EVERY ANGLE

As much as we may be poor at assessing our own shortcomings, that does not mean that, by definition, we are all brilliant at assessing others. Of course, that then means that not everybody will be brilliant at assessing you. Just because someone may be more senior to you, that does not mean they will have all the solutions to your problems. Indeed, when you are in a leadership position, the most valuable feedback will regularly come from your subordinates.

As a result, it is necessary to be open to 360 evaluations, no matter what point you are at in your career or what position you hold. It can help to look to entrepreneurs for inspiration. For this group of executives, every day is a 360 review, because they live and die based on how they are faring with customers, employees, and any other stakeholders. As a cog in a company machine, it is eminently possible to coast along pretty nicely if you're intelligent and hardworking, because your work is unlikely to fall below the acceptable. But it can be hugely beneficial to cultivate an environment in which you are regularly seeking and receiving feedback that ensures your work is more than just acceptable.

Because to become outstanding you need to look at yourself from every angle, that necessity remains even when you reach the top. It is important to note that there is a wrong way to do a 360 review, and that implementation and execution are crucial if the developmental benefits of the process are to be optimised. But being open to them is crucial, because you are the least reliable person to evaluate yourself. As a *Harvard Business Review* article on the subject puts it: "For a GPS system to get an accurate picture of your location, it requires four different satellites. For leaders to get an accurate picture of their own effectiveness, they need feedback from their manager, peers, direct reports, and others in the organization."[4]

FIND A GUIDE

A 360 degree review is an exhaustive and exhausting process. To be open and responsive to them, you need to have a good deal of the resilience we discussed earlier. But you can't, and shouldn't, have them that regularly.

The 360 review is not the only opportunity to get constructive feedback, though. Personal, individual feedback is equally useful, especially when it comes from someone more experienced, more qualified, and more objective than you are. This is where mentors and coaches come in.

The value of a good mentor is obvious. (I mean, just look at what Yoda did for Luke Skywalker!) But seriously, having someone (or many people) to turn to for their advice, their expertise, and their different perspective – or just having someone to bounce ideas off – is invaluable when it comes to gaining self-awareness. A good mentor will pick you up if you're down, but will also keep you in check if you're getting carried away. They'll expose you to new ideas, help you analyse decisions both big and small, and will oftentimes provide opportunities and connections you otherwise wouldn't have got.

The key thing to realise about mentors is they often need to be sought out. Some people get lucky and get taken under someone's wing. But you can also make it happen yourself. You just need to ask.

★

If you want to avoid following the car in front, feedback is a phenomenal ally, so embrace it. If it's something you've avoided up to now, change that. Because to be successful, you need to be self-aware, you need to know how to improve yourself.

It was a theme of all the executive interviews I carried out for this book. Nobody cruises to the top by themselves. Nobody is the finished article on day 1, and the only way to improve is to have other people tell you how.

Capita's Jonathan Lewis puts it this way: "Self awareness is all about learning to turn a mirror on yourself. Whether that's 360s, whether that's coaching sessions, whether that's mentoring sessions. People are not maximally effective in the contribution they can make to their organisation – and/or therefore the progression of their careers – so long as they might have limiting attributes or behaviours that are holding them back. It's a conversation people so often don't want to have. But there needs to be more of it."

So have the conversations. Identify the blemishes. Look in the mirror.

NOTES

1 www.quizz.biz/uploads/quizz/868280/6_7p474.jpg
2 Justin Kruger and David Dunning (1999). Unskilled and Unaware of It: How Difficulties in Recognizing One's Own Incompetence Lead to Inflated Self-Assessments. *Journal of Personality and Social Psychology*, Vol. 77, No. 6, pp. 1121–1134.
3 www.poetryfoundation.org/poems/44301/ode-on-a-distant-prospect-of-eton-college
4 https://hbr.org/2012/09/getting-360-degree-reviews-right

WHERE THE RUBBER HITS THE ROAD

So far we have been dealing with context – generational, societal, professional, and personal scenarios that define who we are and how we get to where we have got to in our lives. The rest of the book now gets into the practical, "self-help" aspect – tools and strategies for avoiding getting stuck behind the car in front.

THREE QUESTIONS

The Japanese have a concept: Ikigai. It means "a reason for being." The word refers to having a meaningful direction or purpose in life, constituting the sense of one's life being made worthwhile, with actions taken towards achieving one's ikigai resulting in satisfaction and a sense of meaning to life.

Many of you will likely be familiar with this and have maybe even used it. Along the way I've picked up a bastardised version (thank you, Dominic Good!) which is simpler and offers a practical framework for helping to make career choices, be that thinking proactively and differently about your next move or finding your way out of the cul-de-sac.

My dumbed-down version involves asking three questions:

1) What do I need?
2) What do I enjoy?
3) What am I good at?

An important element is to see these as entirely interdependent (imagine they are three pins on a board connected by a piece of string. If you pull one of the pins, at least one other has to change the position).

Ikigai

A Japanese concept meaning 'a reason for being'

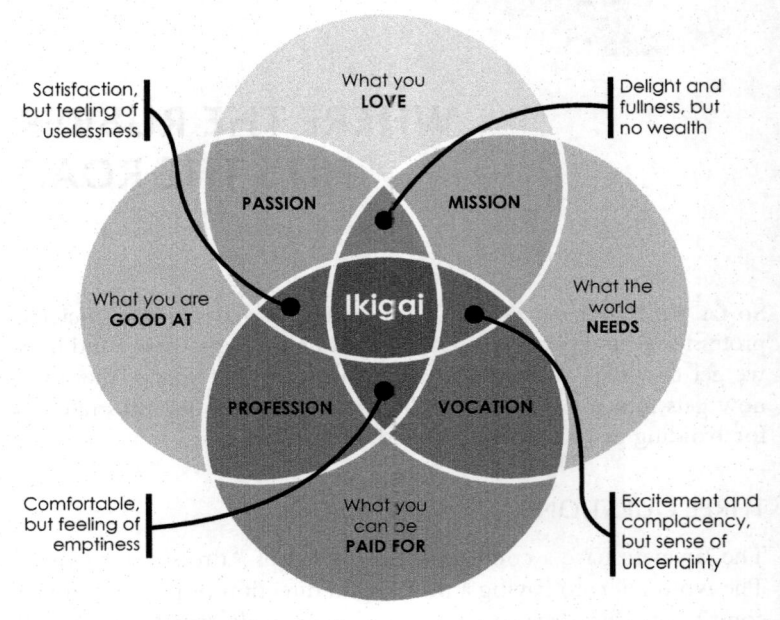

Figure 8.1 The concept of ikigai

I say this because there are trade-offs. For example, if you have critical financial commitments, you will need to earn money which in turn may not be compatible with doing something you totally enjoy. So think about your work life in the context of those three questions when it comes to the next opportunity:

What do you **NEED**? Is it money ("I have three sets of school fees to pay"), is it status ("I need to be the boss"), or is it purpose ("I want to do something worthwhile, I want to get off the treadmill")?

What do you **ENJOY**? Think about a job or situation which gave you genuine pleasure and satisfaction. How did it make you feel? What were the components? What was the context? Now try and crystallise those.

What are you **GOOD AT**? This is more complex to unpack. Most executives get to a point in their career where they have been successful almost by a process of osmosis. This happens with great athletes. Tennis legend Roger Federer talks about how he cannot really explain why his crosscourt forehands are so immaculate. They are effortless, but he can't deconstruct them. Lots of successful business people are the same. They reach the top because they're good and get promoted but often without really fully understanding why.

The other factor to consider at this juncture is the myth of leadership: the idea that to be a leader you have to be good at everything, know everything, and have no weaknesses. Much has been talked about authentic leadership where it is in fact a strength to show your Achilles Heel. (Or as Stevie Spring puts it: "[Having] the confidence of saying, 'I don't know, but I know a man who does'.") But that is subtle, requiring bucketloads of self-awareness, not to mention being risky in a political and cutthroat organisation.

The reality of course is that nobody is good at everything. What many leaders are good at is masking or compensating for weaknesses, which can mean losing sight of genuine strengths.

But if you're thinking of a change of direction, it really is important to rediscover those strengths and be honest about those weaknesses, because you can then isolate those strengths and convert them into capabilities that are transferable into a new sector or a new career. We will go on the explore this concept later in this chapter.

TIMING YOUR RUN

When is the best time to change your job or even your career? A quick Google of this question throws up some obvious answers. "You dread going to work," "you constantly complain about your job," "you don't fit in with the workplace culture," and "your health is being impacted." Yes, if any of these apply to you, it's time to look elsewhere. But hopefully you already knew that.

Then there are the natural moments; the organic endpoints we've already covered in *Into the Cul-de-Sac*. A new boss arrives with a different agenda, your company comes under economic pressure and cost-cutting/voluntary redundancies loom, there is a merger where your role is duplicated. Or maybe you simply feel unfulfilled or unhappy.

Another slightly more subtle answer to this question is that you should leave when you're no longer learning. Even if you're still enjoying your job, if most days are the same and you feel that you could carry out your duties with your eyes shut, it's probably time to leave. Not just for your sake but for the company's. Because, as Impala CMO Caroline Hudack notes, if you're no longer learning and you're apathetic at work, "you're not bringing energy, and you're not bringing new ideas, and you're not bringing the optimism that the company needs."

The problem with all the previous scenarios, even the last one to an extent, is that they all come too late. They're panic departures, if you will. You've run out of road and you've got no room for manoeuvre. Leaving a job or changing career in this type of situation is limiting, even though it may often be necessary.

SURFING THE SIGMOID CURVE

Perversely, the best time to move on is when it's all going really well. You are at the top of your game, you can do no wrong, and you're looking at the next promotion. That's the time to leave, when there's still lots of roads ahead of you.

This mindset is perfectly encapsulated in the concept of the sigmoid curve. A sigmoid function is a mathematical function having a characteristic "S"-shaped curve or sigmoid curve, like this one:

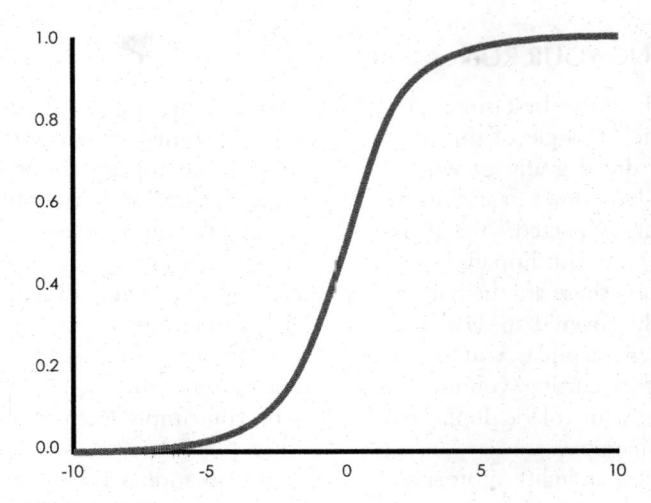

Figure 8.2 A sigmoid curve

It can be applied in lots of different ways. For example, in the natural world, simple organisms can demonstrate the phases of a sigmoidal growth curve. After an initial lag period, there will be a period of exponential growth while resources remain abundant. Then when resources become limited, the growth rate may begin to slow, before eventually plateauing. Because organisms are being grown in closed systems, an accumulation of metabolic waste will inevitably occur, and this will eventually lead to an increase in the rate of death and an overall reduction in population size.

What, you might ask, has this got to do with careers? Well, the sigmoid curve is a perfect representation of so many executive roles and careers. At the start, you're learning the ropes, bedding in, establishing yourself, and building relationships. But despite all the work you're doing, you don't initially progress that far and certainly not fast. Like a germinating seed, though, you are laying the foundation for what will eventually come your way: a rapid process of growth. The promotions start coming, the salary goes up, the office gets bigger, and the job title more prestigious. What the sigmoid curve shows us is that that growth doesn't continue ad infinitum. It will eventually plateau and can then decline.

Simply being aware of this – that the good times don't last forever – and knowing where you are on your own sigmoid curve is a good start. But the most successful executives go even further. They jump off the curve when it is still on the up but approaching its peak, and they start on the bottom of another curve. They know that, although this can be tough and may mean more difficult times ahead at the bottom of a new curve, in the long run, it gets you ahead of those who simply ride the first wave to its completion. Basically, you want to do this:

And then do it again and again, because, as has already been addressed, the path to the top is not straightforward. It's not A to B. It's not even A to B to C. It's all the letters of the Latin alphabet, the Greek alphabet, the Russian alphabet, and any other alphabet you care to think of. "It's very important to know where you're going," says Sophie Adelman, co-founder and CEO of The Garden, "but be flexible enough to take opportunities." You have to be prepared to quit while you're ahead, reinvent yourself, take risks, stand up to new challenges, and push through the tricky times to reap the rewards.

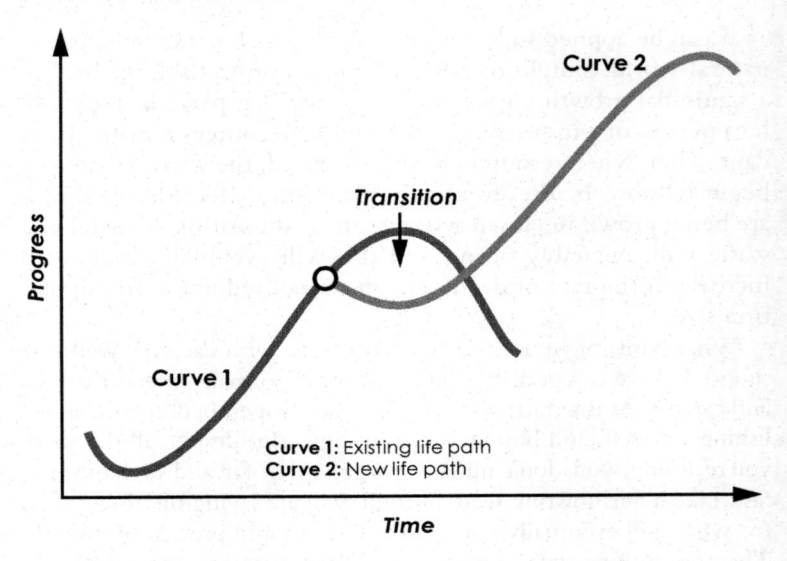

Figure 8.3 Surfing sigmoid curves

So the best advice I can give you on when to change jobs is to do it before you think you have to. Always assume that the first curve is nearing a peak, so that you can prepare for the new curve to get underway. Because preparing for the second curve too early is far better than waiting until it is too late and the plateau/decline has set in.

Some of the smartest executives I've come across are those that successfully surf the sigmoid curve. Think Adam Crozier arriving as chief executive of ITV in 2010 when the business was on its knees in the aftermath of the global credit crunch and leaving the business in 2017 in amazing shape having led a successful turnaround (before the pressures of streamers such as Netflix and Amazon Prime really began to bite) or Dave Lewis announcing his departure from Tesco after overseeing a five-year turnaround from a financial crisis and an accounting scandal that almost shredded the grocer's blue-chip reputation. Perhaps the shareholders weren't quite so happy at these decisions, but both Crozier and Lewis left on a high to jump on the next curve. And indeed, that's not a bad way to look at things. If others aren't that happy you're leaving, you're probably making the right move.

GETTING OUT OF THE CAR

But what if you've not got out at the right time? In *Into the Cul de Sac* I talked about the fact that many people do end up, often inadvertently, stuck in a one-way street, or worse, in a dead end. Anyone who has actually driven into a dead end will know that it's very tricky to reverse out, in particular if another car has followed you in.

So what do you do in that situation? All the sigmoid curves in the world are not going to help you with that problem. I can speak from first-hand experience on this topic.

By the mid-2000s I had been in advertising for the best part of 25 years. But a combination of "Groundhog Day" (every problem, every situation was one I'd seen many times before), the somewhat infantilising effect of arguing with marketing managers about the size of the logo in a press ad, and the slow demise of advertising as the digital revolution gathered pace led me to the point that I was losing interest, but more worryingly, losing my mojo as an ad man. In any business, that is a very dangerous place to be because to be at the top of a company you have to be at the top of your game. I could see that there would be a time in the next few years where I would get called out. I was 48 and really did not want this to be happening in my early 50s. (I had seen far too many once-successful ad men humiliatingly holding on by their fingertips.) That was the point I decided to get out, even though I didn't have a plan.

The problem was that when I made the decision to leave the advertising profession, I had no real idea what I wanted to do. A somewhat disturbing discovery was that the skills that advertising taught you were applicable to, well, advertising.

Consequently, I kept a very open mind and found myself doing advisory work in the private equity world (such as working as a non-executive director for small high-growth digital businesses). I was approached by a former ad agency colleague who was setting up a boutique executive search firm for the advertising sector. I joined them in start-up mode working out of the Hospital Club with laptops perched on the corners of coffee tables. It was then that the penny dropped. I could see the transferable skills and competencies (covered in more detail in the next section) that I had accrued – pitching to clients, project managing the process from writing a brief to delivering a candidate (not dissimilar to delivering a campaign), and building and nurturing relationships. However, I realised that I did not want to do it in a firm focusing on the advertising industry which I was trying to escape from. So I began approaching the big international executive search firms. Bear in mind this was early 2008 and the dark clouds of the Credit Crunch were looming. Most executive search firms were pulling down the shutters, but Spencer Stuart, unbeknownst to me, had been looking for some time for someone to rebuild their Media Practice and I fitted the bill. I joined in August 2008 (one month before Lehmans went down!) and I haven't looked back since.

So what did I learn from that experience? Well, apart from the fact that I wish I had read a book like this, three things:

1) **Don't panic**
   The inevitable fear of finding yourself trapped is to find a solution as soon as possible. If you're in a job in this situation, you have a degree of luxury in that you are being paid while you look for something new (although don't underestimate the stress of leading a double life – sneaking off early to do an interview or awkward calls in the open plan area). If, as was the case for me, you leave your job without a job, there will be an overwhelming desire to find something quickly. My response to that is not to rush, buy yourself time. The problem with rushing is twofold. First, you could end up 'panic buying' and taking a job without thinking it through properly. (Is the role really as advertised? Have you looked under the bonnet of the company's financials? Is it the right cultural fit?) Second, fear is palpable. Interviewers will sense immediately that you're worried or desperate. It's not a good look. Ideally give yourself three to six months, even 12 months if you have the financial wherewithal. That will give you the time and space to make the right decision and to convey confidence.

2) **Keep an open mind**
   Of course, it's only natural to want to be focused and targeted. A career spent moving seamlessly from one role to the next will condition you to expect a linear career trajectory. But alongside giving yourself time should also come being open to experimentation. Talk to as wide a range of people as you can, ideally outside of the network within which you have operated. Every

time you have a conversation with a contact, ask them for the name of someone else you ought to meet. Even if an idea seems crazy, still take the meeting. Two things will happen. Your network will grow exponentially and you will start to encounter people and companies outside of your comfort zone (and you may be surprised at how interesting they are). Second, each one of these conversations is a data point. Think of them as dots in a Georges Seurat painting: in time, shapes will emerge that may give you a new and intriguing perspective on the next opportunity. And by the way, don't feel anxious about taking on advisory or consultancy projects. They too will add new dimensions to your experience and may even be your next full-time job. People also get worried that they might get offered a new role whilst consulting. Think of it as the same as a three- or six-month notice period which is what an employer would have had to accept were you in full-time employment.

3) **Be systematic**

Treat this process like a full-time project. Assemble the names of everyone you have worked or connected with and then refine it to the 20 or 30 you feel you really rate or are in interesting positions. Don't be embarrassed to contact them. At the same time, don't let them feel that this is an exercise in "give us a job." Instead, appeal to their good nature and/or ego by saying that you want to ask their advice. Never leave a conversation without having learnt something new or getting the name of someone else you should talk to. You will need to drink lots of cups of coffee, but the benefits will be manifold. In my experience, 50% of the time, someone's next job comes from their network rather than the services of a headhunter.

That all being said, it's probably best not to end up in my situation. I was lucky enough to find my second career by getting out of the car, but you would be far better off getting ahead of the curve. Read on.

COMPETENCIES NOT CURRICULUM VITAE (OR TURNING YOUR CV INSIDE OUT)

Most people like a good list: a to-do list, a shopping list, and a bucket list.

This is effectively what a CV is – a list of jobs. From the time we sit down with the school careers adviser, we are encouraged to write a CV – a record of organisations worked in and roles. As we go on in the world of work, this becomes more elaborate and impressive.

The problem is that it remains a list of the WHAT and misses the critical component of the HOW, which is why most professional job interviews are driven by the competency-based model where the employer really wants to know whether you have the right skills to take the position on, rather than being focused solely on your experience or previous qualifications. So rather than concerning themselves with the 'what' of past achievements, they place emphasis on the "how" – your competencies.

Thus, any self-respecting HR Director will ask you questions that start with: "Tell me a time when . . . Can you think of an example of how/when . . . Describe a way in which you."

A surprising number of people are simply not ready for this type of questioning and stumble with the answers.

More fundamentally, however, understanding your competencies is a critical factor in helping you identify what your transferable skills are. These are the skills that will create the bridge from your current role in your current company in your current sector to a new role in a new company in a new sector.

Genuinely understanding your competencies and what you have to offer is not necessarily an easy thing to do, even for the most experienced executives. Take Jonathan Lewis. Jon spent the first decade of his career as an academic – carrying out research for the oil and gas industry – after becoming passionate about geology at Kingston Polytechnic, as was, in the early 1980s. (He also has a PhD from the University of Reading.) Since moving into the corporate world in 1996, he has earned himself a reputation as a turnaround guru for struggling businesses. The talent he has for effecting turnarounds and his necessary up-for-the-challenge attitude are underpinned, he says, by abilities, he honed during his time as an academic, because as an academic, as a scientist, everything he did involved deconstructing problems and breaking them down into digestible parts. A grounding in getting to the nub of a problem – and then having his methods challenged by his academic peers and superiors – armed Lewis with the skills he needed to get where he is today. He freely admits, though, that it was a headhunter that first made this connection for him, not something he identified himself.

A clear and compelling explanation (as mentioned earlier) of your transferable skills helps employers understand why your experiences gained in a utility will be useful to an airline. (In the subsequent section, *Exploring your Solar System*, we look at sector mobility in more detail.)

The secret is to turn your CV, and thus your career narrative, inside out. What were the key moments during your career where you exhibited key competencies?

Competencies are the skills and behaviours required for success.[1] Competency definitions are pretty common currency in the talent industry as a way of identifying the skills and behaviours required for success. For example, global human capital firm, Korn Ferry, has a sophisticated yet understandable and practical approach to identifying competencies as part of their Four Dimensional Executive Assessment process (KF4D-Exec).[2]

It sets out four broad "factors" – Thought, Results, People, and Self – and attributes to them a number of competencies (along with helpful descriptions). These are what you should focus on. Typically you would select four or five that best sum up your strengths as an executive. For example, you might be a natural diplomat who is skilled at "balancing the needs of multiple stakeholders" (i.e., *balances stakeholders*). Or you are disciplined and outcome-oriented, which means you are good at "holding yourself and others accountable for meeting commitments" (i.e., *ensures accountability*). Or perhaps you are one of those people who are comfortable with trial and error (something, by the way, that all high-growth tech businesses prize as a key competency). In which case you are likely to "actively learn through experimentation, using both successes and failures as learning fodder" (i.e., *Nimble learning*).

Use these competencies as a framework to then describe the HOW of your achievements, using the evidence (facts and figures and resulting outcomes) to bring the competencies to life. This will become your "narrative" for an interview or, as you will see further on in this section, the rich content for your CV.

FACTOR	COMPETENCY	DEFINITION
Thought	*Balances stakeholders*	Anticipating and balancing the needs of multiple stakeholders
	Cultivates innovation	Creating new and better ways for the organisation to be successful
	Global perspective	Taking a broad view when approaching issues, using a global lens
	Strategic vision	Seeing ahead to future possibilities and translating them into breakthrough strategies
Results	*Aligns execution*	Planning and prioritising work to meet commitments aligned with organisational goals
	Ensures accountability	Holding self and others accountable for meeting commitments
People	*Develops talent*	Developing people to meet both their career goals and the organisation's goals
	Engages and inspires	Creating a climate in which people are motivated to do their best to help the organisation achieve its objectives
	Manages conflict	Handling conflict situations effectively, with a minimum of noise
	Navigates networks	Effectively building formal and informal relationships inside and outside the organisation
	Persuades	Using compelling arguments to gain the support and commitment of others
Self	*Courage*	Stepping up to address difficult issues, saying what needs to be said
	Manages ambiguity	Operating effectively, even when things are not certain or the way forward is not clear

	Nimble learning	Actively learning through experimentation when tackling new problems, using both successes and failures as learning fodder
	Situational adaptability	Adapting approach and demeanour in real time to match shifting demands of different situations

One additional observation is that I am continually surprised by how regularly experienced, smart executives struggle to put together a compelling CV. Sometimes this is because they have moved effortlessly from one role or company to another without having to proactively search. There has simply been no need to write a CV. This is particularly the case where the individual has been innocently following the car in front and suddenly found themselves sitting in that fateful cul-de-sac. At this point, it's really important to stand back and look in a different way at your career and your achievements – a kind of "out of body experience."

Here are some helpful tips on how to structure a good CV that shine a light on the HOW as much as the WHAT.

As we have already seen, the critical element of a good CV is your competencies. This doesn't mean to say that you do not feature a classic chronological career journey, but you will prioritise and order it in a different way. These are harder to write but are likely to be more impactful.

The structure will look something like this:

> **Name and contact details:** should include your home address, your mobile number, and private email address. Sounds pretty obvious but you really don't want a busy HR executive losing the will to live looking for your contact details buried somewhere in your CV.

> **Personal profile:** a short, well-crafted paragraph that summarises you as an executive, ideally written in the third person, e.g., "*International marketing professional with a combination of commerciality and creativity. Experience gained in operating in the blue-chip consumer goods sector both the USA and Europe . . . etc.*" You get the picture.

Key competencies: three or four examples of situations where you have delivered outcomes or results in the kinds of categories set out earlier, e.g., *"Strategic Vision – Over a period of three years at BigCo during which the business was undergoing significant structural disruption, a critical task was to pivot the sales function from a traditional field marketing approach to a scalable, digital sales platform. In my role as Chief Revenue Officer, I was responsible for this major strategic shift, introducing and implementing Salesforce CRM in parallel with reconfiguring and rebuilding the salesforce. The result was an improved sales performance of 25 percent without impacting on our Net Promoter Score."* That kind of thing.

Career history: in reverse chronological order, a list of your roles and the companies where you worked with a short, bullet-point description of key facts: size and scope of the division, team size and composition, geographical coverage, and projects/tasks delivered under your watch.

Awards, citations, non-executive directorships: a short summary with the most recent or relevant examples first.

Education and qualifications: Ditto.

References: optional and very much depends on your current situation. If you are gainfully employed, then probably not sensible to encourage a situation where your name is being openly linked to an opportunity. However, if you are "resting," then two or three significant referees will look reassuring.

EXPLORING YOUR SOLAR SYSTEM

Everyone starts somewhere. Post-education the search for your first job sees you starting in a company which in turn sits within a sector.

As we've explored previously, the priority tends to be simply getting a job. Some with vocational degrees steer effortlessly into related careers as lawyers, engineers, or doctors. Some with a clear eye (or maybe some helpful family connections) end up in their dream job. The majority, however, end up in a job through a mixture of happenstance, luck, and a bit of judgement.

Consequently, many people grow up learning a trade in a particular sector and, in tune with the premise of this book, run the danger of following the car in front for too many years.

Many executives struggle with the concept of how skills forged over years in a particular company or in a particular sector might be transferable to a different sector. Executives in functional roles – Finance, Marketing, Technology, and Legal – find this easier in that they have sets of skills for which the read-across is very clear for everyone to see (every business needs a finance director, a head of marketing, an IT director, or a brief).

But frequently I find myself having to help people, even functional experts, with advice on how their experience might be applicable to a completely new sector, let alone a new company. At the heart of this lies the advice set out in *Competencies not Curriculum Vitae*.

Once again, this is an approach that can be used whether you are proactively looking for a change or have found yourself stuck on a career tramline which is heading inevitably for the terminus.

An additional exercise is thinking about which sectors would be most relevant. In short, where are the adjacencies? Rather like planets in the solar system, the closer the planet the closer the connection, and of course the further the planet, the longer and more challenging the journey.

Having a real grasp of your competencies is the first important plank of transferability. The next is analysing sector trajectory or "white space" and understanding whether your strengths are a fit.

Here are some examples.

We are going through a period where, thanks to the internet, customer engagement and personalisation are an increasingly critical factor in business growth and success. So if you are working in a sector with significant e-commerce credentials like retail, you are likely to be highly prized by a sector like consumer packaged goods (think soap powder, instant noodles, and chocolate bars), which isn't able to connect or sell directly to consumers but increasingly needs to.

Or you are working in a "born digital" business in a highly disrupted sector like travel (think Booking.com or AirBnB). Your skills in harnessing consumer data and building algorithmic solutions for customer engagement will be needed in a traditional sector that is going through a significant disruption such as TV or newspaper publishing, who need to quickly build skills in subscription.

Perhaps you come from the consumer services world (say, utilities or telecoms) where your customer base is a mix of large enterprises, SMB (small- to medium-sized businesses), and mass consumers; and where customer acquisition and retention are second nature. You could be extremely valuable to the healthcare sector, which is increasingly having to engage directly with patients, as well as going through intermediaries such as physicians or healthcare organisations, like the NHS.

Or maybe you work in a highly regulated sector such as financial services where you are used to creating services or marketing programmes that still have impact despite the constraints of regulation. You would be very valuable in business sectors that are under the spotlight from a regulatory point of view such as gaming or, increasingly, the social media platforms.

There isn't a science to this – it's more about finding the "red thread" that connects one role or sector to another. But by establishing which of your neighbouring planets are easily accessible, the potential options for the future of your career can multiply significantly.

All these exercises are valuable in coming to a genuine understanding of what you have to offer. It will help you advance from relying on the **WHAT** of your CV, to having a compelling explanation of the **HOW** of your competencies.

But that's only half the job; the next step is being able to accurately pitch your **WHO**.

NOTES

1 Michael M. Lombardo and Robert W. Eichinger (2009). *FYI: For Your Improvement, a Guide for Development and Coaching* (5th ed.). Lominger International.
2 © Korn Ferry 2016. All rights reserved. Korn Ferry's Four Dimensional Executive Assessment.

DEFINING YOUR ARCHETYPE

Please indulge this throwback to my time in advertising, where the job was about building clearly-etched, long-term brand equities; and where strong brands had an advantage in their market which led to increased growth, market share, and profitability.

I do believe that part of being a successful executive is having a clear brand. It is not about over-simplifying the complexity and depth of an individual's personality; rather, it is about recognising fundamental strengths and bringing them to the fore.

So, ask yourself, what kind of person are you?

OH, TO BE JUNG

Brand consultancy Haines McGregor has created a really engaging model to help locate and understand the relationship between different professional personalities. Founder Jeremy Haines rooted this in the thinking of Carl Jung, one of the founding fathers of analytical psychology and the inventor of the concept of "archetypes."

Jung theorised that, at birth, the human mind (or psyche) is not a blank slate. Nor is each individual human mind exclusively the product of personal experience. According to Jung, there exist "identical psychic structures common to all [humans]."[1] He called these structures "archetypes," a collection of primitive mental images and narratives inherited from the earliest human ancestors.

These archetypes are housed in what Jung termed the "collective unconscious" (as distinct from an individual's "personal unconscious"). And it is because of the collective unconscious that we instinctively recognise these archetypes. For Jung, the influence of archetypes on human thought and behaviour explains the similarities in patterns, themes, and symbols evident in the myths and religions of multiple cultures throughout history.

He wrote: "From the unconscious emanate determining influences which, independently of tradition, guarantee in every single individual a similarity and even a sameness of experience, and also of the way it is represented imaginatively. One of the main proofs of this is the almost universal parallelism between mythological motifs."[2]

As evidence of their universality and cultural pervasiveness, let's take a look at the "hero" archetype. The most ancient literary work we have, predating the *Iliad* and the oldest biblical texts, is the Epic of Gilgamesh. An epic poem from ancient Mesopotamia that dates back over 4,000 years, it was unearthed in 1853 by archaeologists, carved onto Babylonian tablets. These tablets were later translated by a young Londoner called George Smith, a self-taught scholar employed at the British Museum who had left school at 14.

The tale that unfolds in the Epic of Gilgamesh, in which the eponymous hero king saves his community from external threats, has a number of parallels in the Old Testament (not least the Genesis flood narrative), in medieval literature (the Legend of King Arthur, Saint George, and the Dragon), and, bringing it more up to date, James Bond, Star Wars, and Harry Potter. In re-telling these stories, we not only reaffirm our beliefs and values but also create a moral framework that helps us recognise what we aspire to or wish to become.

This mode of thinking has proved to be as widely applicable today as ever in disciplines such as personality diagnosis, market research, recruitment, and numerous other spheres. And its validity has proved remarkably robust.

BRAND YOU

Haines McGregor has cleverly adapted this concept of archetypes to create a framework for codifying professional identities. By placing the various archetypes onto a map (see Figure 9.1), it is possible to understand how each one relates to the others.

The horizontal axis is to do with how we fit into society and its culture, from more sociable to more independent and individualistic. The vertical, personality axis is more extrovert at the top and

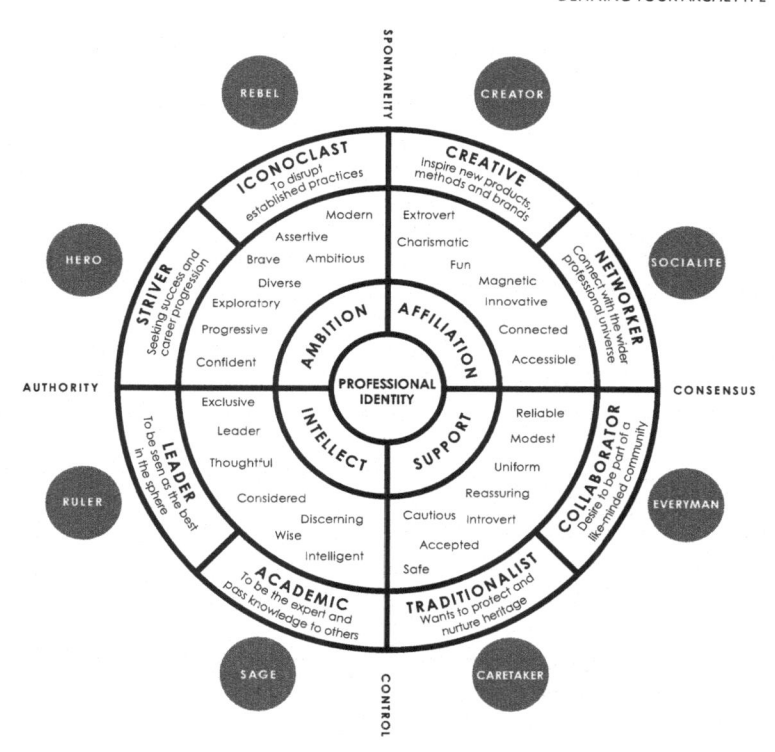

Figure 9.1 Haines McGregor archetypes wheel

introvert at the bottom. This is sometimes referred to as the life and death axis; which is to say open to living at the top and afraid of death at the base. This is, of course, symbolic rather than actual, but nevertheless, we will all have been aware of occasions when we want to be carefree and uninhibited, as contrasted with a desire to have everything in our lives neat and tidy and under control. It's important to note that there's no bad place to be on the map; they are all part of the human condition. Indeed, we may behave differently in different circumstances, but for the purposes of answering the question of who I am and what do I want to be, it's useful to understand the place where you predominate as well as some of the tensions created by the other archetypes.

From four core drivers – Ambition, Affiliation, Support, and Intellect – eight archetypes emerge.

If your professional identity is based on *Intellect*, then you might define yourself on the one hand as a Leader (to be seen as the best in the sphere) or an Academic (to be the expert and pan knowledge in others). As the former, your archetype is the RULER; as the latter, you are a SAGE. Or maybe *Affiliation* is at your core. This would lead to two archetypes: the Creative (CREATOR) who inspires new products, methods, and brands, or the Networker (SOCIALITE), connecting with the wider professional universe.

Interestingly, there are also "dark" sides to these archetypes. (Star Wars creator George Lucas has been heavily influenced by archetypal thinking. The concept of the "dark" side, the struggle of good versus evil, and people being lured in and out of different personas, is not far short of a treatise on archetypal characters.) When under pressure, or perhaps when over-confident, people can appear as exaggerated versions of themselves. As a RULER, you may fall foul of pretension, as the SAGE, a tendency towards obsessiveness. As the CREATOR, you may be a bit risky to work with; as the SOCIALITE, you may be insincere.

Take a look at the professional identity wheel and think about where your emphasis lies. Then let's link those to the Korn Ferry competencies we talked about in the previous chapter:

The Iconoclast	=	Courage
The Striver	=	Situational adaptability
The Ruler	=	Engages and inspires
The Sage	=	Strategic vision
The Caretaker	=	Manages conflict
The Everyman	=	Situational adaptability
The Socialite	=	Navigates networks
The Creator	=	Cultivates innovation

This approach can take you deeper than a merely superficial identity. It helps you answer the initial question of "What do I think I am like?" But it also leads you into other interesting questions: what do I aspire to be like? What do I want to avoid being like? What do I fear most that I might become?

It is often the case that these drivers and archetypes appear contradictory and people tend to operate on an axis rather than only ever being one thing. For example, someone may predominate in a certain alignment, such as a buttoned-down control freak, in the workplace, whilst being a thrill-seeker at the weekend. We move in and out, more so today than ever before, of different modes, depending on context.

★

What's the value of this exercise? As we see from the previous example, human beings are complex, textured. Add to that an individual's career journey and the picture becomes a veritable Rubik's Cube.

But in a world of soundbites, of Snapchat and TikTok, of 30-second TV commercials, it is the case that our brains are increasingly wired to seek shortcuts, to judge a book by its cover. Consequently, it's important to have a clear understanding of your "short form," your brand personality. What do you stand for? What is your value system?

The exercise in this section is a start-point to boiling that down to an essence which isn't just whimsical but is linked to the hard metrics of your competencies as an executive. Once you have that, it becomes a whole lot easier to make intelligent, productive progress, even if it may move you into a whole new sector. It also makes it much easier to pitch yourself to other people.

NOTES

1 www.harleytherapy.co.uk/counselling/carl-jung-archetypes.htm#
2 *Collected Works of C.G. Jung, Volume 9 (Part 1): Archetypes and the Collective Unconscious.* Princeton University Press.

10

GET OUT MORE

Networking. Even nowadays, this is a word that makes people shudder (particularly if you're British). It conjures up images of walking into a room full of hundreds of people who you've never met before, plunging in, shaking hands, flashing white teeth, and doling out business cards like they're going out of fashion (which, in fact, they might be). Or that moment at a conference when it comes to the Q&A and you desperately cast about for that insightful question. (Don't worry, Ron Meadows from Ron Meadows Consulting puts his hand up and the moment has gone.)

The bad news is that you cannot avoid it. If you want to be a successful executive, you have to be an effective networker – not least because that's how the top positions are filled. "I always talk to people about the importance of connections," says Facebook's Carrie Timms, "because you never know how your connections will often play out." Timms speaks from experience having moved client-side from agency roles early on in her career by drawing on her network. "Once I decided that I wanted to move," she explains, "I thought, I'm going to use my network and get advice from people who have successfully done this." That active choice and smart networking, combined with the always crucial "bit of serendipity," led to Timms successfully making a significant career move.

As far back as 1999, the received wisdom was that as many as 70–80% of the best jobs came from effective, consistent networking.[1] That figure hasn't changed much over the last two decades. A 2016 survey found "85 percent of critical jobs are filled via networking of some sort."[2] For better or worse, it really is about who you know, not what you know.

But there is good news: networking is not necessarily what you think. Yes, one element is the conference circuit, boldly diving in at big events where you don't know anyone and trying to forge meaningful, beneficial connections. But that is only a very small element (and likely to diminish further in a post-COVID world). Thankfully for the introverts out there, networking as a whole is much more multilayered. There are plenty of other ways to do it effectively.

KEEP IT CLEAN

The truth is that professional networking makes most of us feel dirty — literally. A 2014 study found a "causal relationship between instrumental networking for professional goals, feeling dirty, and [the] need for cleansing."[3] As a result, many of us avoid networking despite knowing that it will be beneficial to our careers. We would certainly cringe at the recommendation to go to more networking events. So, how do you network without needing a shower afterwards?

David Burkus, author of *Friend of a Friend . . . Understanding the Hidden Networks That Can Transform Your Life and Your Career*, believes networking needs to be redefined. Forget about meeting strangers. Instead, realise the potential of the network that's already around you.

To do this, Burkus makes three recommendations[4]:

1) Get in touch with old friends or weak/dormant ties, as sociologists would call them — old school friends, former colleagues, and one-time team-mates. When you see them, don't have an agenda — it's the agenda-ness of networking that makes so many of us awkward in the first place. Just see where it goes. And after you've said, "this was fun, we should do it again," actually do it again.
2) Use current friends to make new friends. When you do have an agenda of sorts — perhaps you want to enter a new industry — use your current connections to make new ones. So ask friends or close colleagues, "Who do you know in _____ or at _____?" The breadth of your network just a degree of separation out from you is huge. And making a connection through someone

else is much easier, and more effective, than trying to make a connection cold.
3) Don't talk to strangers . . . about work. When you do meet a new person — whether it be at a networking event or just a friend's dinner party — don't ask them: "So, what do you do?" Ask them about passions and hobbies; find non-work interests. You will form deeper relationships much faster that way. And a friend is a much stronger connection in a network than a work acquaintance.

Alongside this advice on how to do basic networking, it is also essential to understand that networking is not just for the bad times. Stay in touch. Even when your career is going well, keeping in touch with your network is hugely important. Perhaps not unsurprisingly, despite a majority (79%) of people globally agreeing that professional networking is valuable for career progression, less than half (48%) say they keep in touch with their network when things are going well in their career.[5] So doing so will separate you from the pack. It will also keep you alive to opportunities that others might not get, a key tenet to avoiding the car in front.

MAKE WAVES

If we call the previously mentioned networking 101 — advice for anyone at any point in their career who finds the process difficult — what follows is the advanced class. Even if you're already good at pressing the flesh and chewing everyone's ear off at a cocktail party, there are ways to do it better — ways to be more focused and structured in your networking to your greater benefit.

John Smith, former chief executive of BBC Worldwide and chief operating officer of Burberry — guided by legendary Korn Ferry alum and coach Peter Hogarth — utilised a number of approaches which brought him out from the shadows of functional leadership as a CFO to become a widely known and respected senior executive.

"You need to **get known**," was the first piece of advice John got from Peter. This can be achieved in a number of ways, but most revolve around thought leadership because you want to get known for the right reasons. You want to be seen as an authority.

The start point is to have a point of view on a subject or an issue which you then amplify in a range of different channels – authoring white papers or articles in business/specialist publications, speaking at conferences, nurturing relationships with key journalists who quote you in exchange for helpful background information, and, of course, effectively utilising the all-important social media (more of which mentioned later).

Allied but distinct to getting known is the need to **widen your circle**. Basically, this means, if you haven't already, expanding your network beyond your own industry, and definitely your own company. Having a limited circle is directly related to following the car in front, because without external influences, you will not even be exposed to the possibilities that lie elsewhere, let alone be able to explore them.

Smith talks about how, by the time he got to the BBC, he had a respectable network of about 100 or so fellow finance executives in the wider business community. It was Peter Hogarth who explained to him that this was not going to be particularly helpful if John wanted to fulfil his ambition of becoming chief executive. He would need to have a reputation and profile beyond the core CFO community.

"Peter said that, in the modern world, any senior executive needs to have a really thorough approach to contacts. You need a lot of them, they need to be respectable. You need to think about different countries, different industries, different job functions, and really work at it. And so I did. And I went from a handful of names to thousands of people in my contact database."

For many like John, this is a mindset issue. Most people have a network beyond their core community but assume that, because they don't share the same professional interest, they are somehow not relevant or interested. Combined with the aforementioned ideas about getting known, you have ample scope to engage with a much wider range of constituencies. Over a period of years, John's expanded network created an ecosystem of relationships and contacts that opened up many doors to both executive and non-executive roles further down the track.

One further way to broaden your network which will open up even more doors is to **become respectable**. In John's case, it was joining the Accounting Standards Board. In my case, it was chairing a panel on behalf of the Advertising Standards Authority (the General Media Panel, a kind of Court of Appeal for advertisers who felt their case needed a second opinion). For others, it could be joining the board of a trade association or becoming a trustee of a not-for-profit.

What's the point here? It's a form of enlightened self-interest. An opportunity to genuinely give something back brings real value to an organisation that needs your wisdom while at the same time positioning you as a person who wants to do the right thing and introduces you to a different community, because that's all networking is: introducing yourself to different communities.

BACK TO SCHOOL

By the time most of us have finished school and maybe university, we've had enough of education. Some go on to do a Masters, while others an MBA. But for the vast majority, education is left behind in favour of learning on the job.

However, there is a time and a place to reconnect with the world of formalised learning. This frequently happens when an executive gets to a career crossroads (as covered in *Into the Cul-de-Sac*). For many (in particular, if the company is happy to fund it), taking time out to participate in an Advanced Management Programme or AMP (think a mini MBA) can be a great opportunity to refresh and recalibrate. All the premium business schools have AMP courses that are tailored to mid-career executives who, because of work and family commitments, cannot take a lot of time off. They vary from four weeks (INSEAD) to three months (Harvard), but all have the same objective in mind: to introduce executives, who have spent their working lives in one sector (or maybe one company), to the very latest in business thinking from a broad range of business categories.

According to the *Financial Times*' 2021 Business School rankings,[6] the top institutions in the world to undertake business learning are as follows:

1) Insead (primary campus France/Singapore)
2) London Business School (UK)
3) The University of Chicago Booth School of Business (US)

4) IESE Business School (Spain)
5) Yale School of Management (US)

There are multiple positive by-products of going back to school, exposing you to a group of fellow students from all over the world and from very different backgrounds (another opportunity to expand your network). Giving you renewed self-confidence thanks to perspectives and strategies you have learned which are much broader than those acquired so far in your career. For many, these courses are life changing (sometimes to an extreme – they have acquired the nickname "the divorce course"!).

On his own experience of going on Harvard Business School's AMP (which promises to "transform proven leaders into global executives"), John Smith says: "It is an amazing experience. It teaches you strategy, teaches you the formalities of leadership, and all the things that you need if you're going to end up being a CEO."

Zillah Byng-Thorne, CEO of Future plc, is another who strongly advocates for a return to school even in the midst of a hectic executive career. In the early 2010s, she got a master's degree in Coaching and Behavioural Change from Henley Management College. "It was brilliant," she says, "because I actually, as a consequence of that, got a lot of executive coaching myself. It was very experiential. That really helped me work through my own career aspirations and goals. But also, it was this sanctuary that you go to every month for two or three days, where I would just go and be engaged completely differently in my brain."

In other words, going back to school, and getting out of the familiar environment of your everyday working life, will give you new insights, new perspectives, new skills, new tools, and new connections. What's not to love?

NOTES

1 http://content.time.com/time/subscriber/article/0,33009,990498,00.html
2 www.linkedin.com/pulse/new-survey-reveals-85-all-jobs-filled-via-networking-lou-adler/
3 Tiziana Casciaro, Francesca Gino and Maryam Kouchaki (2014). The Contaminating Effects of Building Instrumental Ties: How Networking Can Make Us Feel Dirty. *Administrative Science Quarterly*, Vol. 59, No. 4, pp. 705–735.

4 www.ted.com/talks/david_burkus_how_to_hack_networking?language=en
5 https://news.linkedin.com/2017/6/eighty-percent-of-professionals-consider-networking-important-to-career-success
6 https://rankings.ft.com/rankings/2859

GOING SOCIAL

As we established in the previous chapter, networking is essential to success. And if you want to network effectively in the 2020s, you need to use social media. Not obsessively. But you do need to use it regularly and properly.

For a certain section of today's workforce, this will seem anathema and potentially trivial. Isn't social media just where people look at cat videos and tell their followers about what they ate for breakfast? Well, no. For better or worse, social media is a serious business now. The days of it being just a silly bit of fun are long gone, as are the days when you could ignore it. Facebook, YouTube, and WhatsApp, the three most popular social networking sites, all have in excess of two billion monthly active users.[1]

THE WHY

From a professional perspective, it is pretty much a given that you should be on social media. It is certainly expected of leaders. According to Brunswick's 2021 Connected Leadership report,[2] by a ratio of higher than five to one, employees prefer to work for a CEO who uses digital and social media, and by a margin of nine to one, financial readers (regular readers of at least two financial news publications) "trust a Connected Leader more than a CEO who does not use social media as part of their work." Additionally, 60% of employees considering joining a company will do part of their research by exploring the CEO's social media accounts. For those between the age of 18 and 24, 82% say they would prefer to work for a CEO who uses social media.

DOI: 10.4324/9781003229308-11

As to the usefulness of social media for an executive, Sree Sreenivasan, one of the world's leading social media scientists, highlights four major areas of opportunity[3]:

- Social media helps you discover new ideas and trends.
- Social media connects you to existing and new audiences in deeper ways.
- Social media brings attention and traffic to your work.
- Through social media, you can build, craft, and enhance your brand.

So there it is. You're expected to be on social media, and there are good reasons for it. For many, particularly younger readers, this will be self-evident, and social media will already play a key role in the way you interact with professional contacts as well as personal ones. But for the committed Luddites out there, this is a tide that is not for turning back. And social media should not be seen as an inconvenience, but as another crucial tool – another weapon in your arsenal.

THE HOW

Telling you that you need to be on social media and why is all well and good. But what about the how of using it effectively? For advice on this, I defer to the superior expertise of Craig Mullaney. Craig is (among many other things) a partner at Brunswick, lead author of their 2021 Connected Leadership report, and one of the leading experts on executives' use of digital and social media to communicate and lead organisations. Here are his five key pieces of advice on how to use social media most effectively in a professional capacity.

1) Start Small – You don't need to go all guns blazing into social media. Just join one site and do it well to start with. Five minutes a day can make a dramatic impact. "When thinking about networking in digital, you've got to choose a social channel to begin with," says Craig. "And LinkedIn is the best place to start." We'll go into more detail about the specifics of LinkedIn later, but the key piece of advice here is: if you haven't already done so, set up a LinkedIn page.

2) Brand Yourself – Don't worry, this has nothing to do with permanently scarring yourself with a branding iron. We've discussed previously in Chapter 9 the importance of crystallising your brand, of being able to communicate what it is you stand for. Social media is unquestionably one of the key forums to express this. So you need to work out what it is you want to project across social media and ensure it remains consistent. "You are presenting your best professional identity on social media," says Craig.

3) Create a Habit – Be consistent with when you use social media for professional purposes. Whether it be daily posts (on most networks this is unnecessary) or weekly posts (perfectly fine), be regular. As well as helping you learn and refine what is and isn't effective, this will also ensure you remain visible. Equally, it is important to get into the habit of connecting with those you meet through old-school networking (i.e., in real life) via social media soon after your initial meeting. "If I've gone to a networking event and come home with 20 business cards," says Craig, "within the next 24 hours, I'm going to identify those individuals' social handles and reach out with a personalised invitation to connect, referencing where we met."

4) Interact – Don't just think about social media as a place to broadcast your thoughts, or post your ideas. It is a place to engage with other users. "This is not a movie theatre, this is a play," says Craig. "There's interaction between the stage and the audience, that's what makes it exciting. You are cultivating a community. And the algorithm rewards that community engagement." And you don't need to post long-form thought leadership to be active on a platform. Short posts, comments, small video clips, and images are all perfectly reasonable ways to begin a conversation and engage others.

5) Be Authentic – You cannot fake it. Your presence on social media has to resonate with who you are. "Probably the number one principle across all content on social media is it has to be authentic," says Craig. What works for one person will not work for others, so you cannot just mimic what a fellow executive is doing. You also can't farm this out. Depending on where you are in your career, you're likely managing your social media yourself. But if you are in a position that someone else is doing

it for you, that staff member needs to have proper access to you. Depending on the outlet, the level of personality you put across will be different, but ensure you always speak like a human; always speak like yourself.

A WORD ON...

LinkedIn – For executives, LinkedIn is unquestionably the biggie. As mentioned earlier, if you're only on one social network, it should be LinkedIn. "It's designed as a professional network," says Craig, "and you can engage without much fear of being trolled and harassed. So it's an easy place to start and a necessary place to start." Many of your colleagues, clients, peers, and prospects will be on LinkedIn. It has 766 million members, ten million of whom are C-suite executives.[4]

The most crucial thing to remember about LinkedIn, says Craig, is that it is a "living resume." So it needs to be an "always-up-to-date reflection of who you are professionally, the value you can add, and where you're going." As a result, you should apply similar rigour to the composition of your LinkedIn profile as you would to the writing of your CV, the essentials of which are covered in Chapter 8. Unlike a physical CV, though, LinkedIn affords you multimedia capabilities. So in the "Featured" section, you can demonstrate your expertise by uploading thought leadership, portfolios, media coverage, and work products. You can display interactive visual and audio content. You can allocate space as needed, ensuring your relevant experiences and skills are prominent while compressing (but not deleting entirely) potentially less relevant information.

When it comes to how you interact on LinkedIn, it's back to the start small advice outlined earlier. You don't have to be publishing sector-defining thought leadership every week. It's enough to add meaningful comments and share things you find interesting, whether it be from other people on the site or from the media. As you grow your community on LinkedIn, this activity will allow you to passively engage with your network in an organic way. If and when you eventually start to develop original content to publish on LinkedIn, you don't need to do your best impression of a *Financial Times* columnist. Short and sweet is fine, and not just in writing. Short videos and audio are a great way to engage others. Let people see and hear as well as read you. Craig's key piece of advice on publishing on LinkedIn is, "don't let the perfect be the enemy of the good." Try things out. See what works. Refine and learn. Don't obsess about the reach of your post. You're building your brand and your community; it will take time. But if you follow the principles set out earlier, it will benefit you hugely.

Instagram – For Craig, "because it's essentially an entirely visual platform, [Instagram] is an ideal place for humanising an executive." As a complement to LinkedIn, it's also a great way to reach "frontline" employees. LinkedIn remains a white-collar platform used by office-based workers. So if your organisation or sector includes non-office-based workers you want to engage, Instagram would be the way to go. Santander's Ana Botin and Walmart's Doug McMillon have both used Instagram effectively for exactly this purpose.

Twitter – In most sectors, Twitter is arguably best avoided. It's hard work and requires a lot of upkeep. To be active on Twitter requires daily activity – rather than weekly on LinkedIn, for example. It is also a tough environment; you have to have thick skin. As has become abundantly clear in the last decade, trolls live on Twitter nowadays, not under bridges. It is a place where mistakes can be made. You need to be very careful about what you're saying, because if you get it wrong, Twitter never forgets. Twitter is effective in influencing two specific audiences, says Craig, which are the media and the political regulatory audience.

Facebook – As with Instagram, Facebook is an effective channel to reach broad audiences. If using for a professional purpose, it is best to have a separate account for this. Many executives will have a profile and friends already, and this is where you can post photos of your nights out, your family holidays, and your stamp collection. Just make sure, as with all social media sites, that your privacy settings are as you want them.

Clubhouse – Craig expects there to be growth in audio as a medium. The benefits are obvious, not least because audio allows for nuanced arguments and discussions, something still sorely lacking from social media. If you're willing to invest the time with regular engagement on Clubhouse or similar, or even your own podcast, it can be fantastically productive. And these kinds of spaces are great for those who don't like to be on camera.

TikTok – You can breathe a sigh of relief, TikTok is unlikely to be a necessary place for executives to engage any time soon. The same is true for Snapchat.

NOTES

1 www.statista.com/statistics/272014/global-social-networks-ranked-by-number-of-users/
2 www.brunswickgroup.com/media/8059/connected-leadership-2021-report.pdf
3 www.nytimes.com/guides/business/social-media-for-career-and-business
4 www.omnicoreagency.com/linkedin-statistics/

THE ENDGAME GAME

Now finally, it's time to ask yourself this question: what does my life look like in 10 years' time? Where do I want to be?

Will you be a public company chief executive? Or do you want to be lying on a beach in the Caribbean? Will you be running your own cheese shop? Or is being a portfolio non-executive director the end goal?

This might seem a trivial exercise, but it's actually quite important. Because whatever the answer is to that question, your career over the next 10 years needs to feature the building blocks that will get you there.

June Felix, CEO of IG Group plc, who originally studied to become a doctor when she was at university, uses a similar method: "One of the things I always say is my favourite class at university was organic chemistry. Organic chemistry is the class that determines whether you get into medical school or not, because that's the wash-out course; it's really difficult."

"But for me, it was all about thinking backwards: where do you want to end up? And then working backwards as to how you get there. Because there are lots of different ways. It's just a question of time and resources. So I apply that to everything."

THE BIG JOB

If your goal is to be a public company CEO, or for that matter any C-level leadership role, this requires a mixture of strategy and tactics. In the conversations with leaders that I have had for this book (and indeed with many leaders over the years), the same list of actions comes back again and again.

A leitmotif throughout this whole book is that human nature would generally encourage you to stay in that comfort zone, in particular if you're successful. But the advice I have heard from so many successful leaders is to take the opportunity when it is offered or becomes available, to do something different, in particular if it allows you to **go beyond the functional skill set,** you have been trained in. Most of us start our career journeys in a specialised role – marketing, finance, strategy, sales, operations, and IT. So at the most general level, the advice here is to broaden your experience.

Martin Glenn, formerly CEO of PepsiCo UK&I, frozen foods business Igloo, United Biscuits, and the Football Association, refers to it as being a "functional tourist." He is a strong advocate of actively seeking out different opportunities be that geographical or sectoral and within that not to turn your nose up at something that might on the surface seem unglamorous, to head towards "the sound of gunfire."

I frequently use the example of Will Orr, a fellow advertising executive who made the jump client-side to join British Gas in marketing, eventually becoming chief marketing officer. I still remember the day he called me and asked for my advice. He had been offered a move to a new role (Managing Director, Home Installations and Smart Metering). This was a £350 million turnover business employing over 2,250 people, many blue-collar workers, and the UK's biggest provider of central heating solutions (boilers to you and me), as well as delivering British Gas' Smart Metering mandate, fitting these meters in all 12 million customers' homes by 2020. This job could not have been more different to his role as a marketing specialist. My response was instant: take it. Why? Because in one fell swoop he would gain invaluable experience of running a real business with a real P&L and finally shake off any lingering perceptions of him as a fluffy marketer. It turned out to be the right decision. He spent three and a half years in the job before being headhunted to join the RAC as Managing Director, and he is now General Manager of Times Newspapers Ltd.

Every one of the CEOs I interviewed for this book discussed the importance of gaining a breadth of experience. There are plenty of people who are happy to do the same thing for most of their working lives. But these people do not become CEOs. And it goes back to being prepared to take some risks, because not every experience will be a good one. But every experience, good or bad, joyful or painful, will add further strings to your bow. Every new experience is a chance to distinguish yourself from others.

In addition, it is helpful to participate in **pan-business initiatives** (M&A, a new product launch). In other words, when there is a project that requires the collaboration of a team of executives from across the functions, this is a great opportunity to understand how your specialism impacts and interacts with the specialisms of others. It will also help you better understand the give-and-take necessary to get an important project across the line successfully. (The best description of collaboration I've heard came from Alexis Nasard – at the time CMO of Heineken – who described true collaboration as "the moment you have to give up something you really value.") Critically, it will teach you how to **integrate and confederate a group of people**, a vital skill needed when you eventually become the single leader who needs to bring everyone with them and to make choices and trade-offs.

Another critical facet is being a **confident contributor to discussions around strategy and finance**, the kinds of things that are debated at the board level. The danger with seeing everything through the eyes of your functional expertise is that choices and decisions can be narrow or self-interested. So this is about looking through the lens of the wider business and setting your thinking in the context of wider commercial value. In short, is what you're recommending really going to deliver value? And that is about being honest with yourself about the pros and cons of an approach to ensure everyone in your organisation, from top to bottom, goes in with their eyes open.

Finally, and as already discussed in *Looking in the Mirror*, **find a mentor** who is already a CEO or in a general management position. This person will be a critical guide and sense-checker when you hit a difficulty or encounter something you've never seen before. Another of my interviewees, Chelsea Football Club chief executive Guy Laurence, is unequivocal on this point. "I don't know anyone who can be successful without mentors," he says. "If you take risks, you sometimes get crises, and you make mistakes. And those are the points you need mentors. They can give you input at critical junctures, plus help you learn from your mistakes. It's not weak to have a mentor, it's weak to think you can survive without one."

YOUR CAPITAL NEED

If 10 years down the line you want to be lying on a beach in the Caribbean, then you're going to need significant capital to support that lifestyle. You're unlikely to get that working your way up the corporate ladder. You're going to need to take a risk: setting up your own business and selling it, or working with private equity on an exit.

Or maybe it's running the cheese shop? Again this is a lifestyle change from the corporate every day, and you'll need to have a learning aptitude. You'll also need to commit to retraining and be unafraid of risk. Along with all the previous points, you will need reserves of capital to see you through the early stages until you have a global chain of cheese shops. Going back to the "Need, Enjoy, Good At" model from *Finding the Balance*, it is likely you will have to initially focus on the Need; that is, roles that deliver high levels of income and capital that can subsequently be ploughed into the business.

GOING PLURAL

And what if your aim is to become one of the good and the great of the non-executive world?

There's a huge amount already written about becoming a non-executive director. All the major executive search firms publish regular surveys and guides. So this section is not in intended to be a comprehensive tool kit but rather to give you some start points for further research. There are also some excellent training courses that will help you with a more in-depth understanding of corporate governance and the regulatory environment (the Financial Times Effective Non-Executive Director Programme is particularly good).

The good news is that boards are increasingly needing to exhibit greater diversity which means that now is an excellent time to be looking at a non-executive appointment, in particular if you represent a diverse perspective. This means that the Catch-22 of needing to have board experience has been loosened to allow first time board directors to be seriously considered.

Obvious as it may sound, the most important question to ask is why do you want to be a non-executive director? The process of building a portfolio will take longer than you think with lots of false starts and hopes. If money is a motivator, then you will be disappointed – non-executive fees are pretty modest. So motivations are more around keeping momentum (and your brain cells) going after an executive career, broadening your network and experiences or "giving something back," be that guiding an executive team or working with a not-for-profit.

It's unlikely you'll secure an FTSE 100 board directorship first time around, so start in the foothills of AIM-listed businesses, earning your spurs as you build your reputation. You will need to give thought to the shape of your portfolio. As already noted, high-profile public company non-executive roles don't pay that well (the average annual fee for an FTSE NXD is around £40,000–50,000), so you might want to amplify this with an Executive Chairman role of an early-stage business where they may pay your salary and also give you a percentage of the equity.

But how do you go about building an NXD career? The first consideration is that, unless you know them, Chairmen or Nominations Committees won't know about you. In other words, finding a directorship is a full-time job in itself. So sit down with a spreadsheet and list the names of all the people you have met who you value, in particular those who are already on the non-executive ladder. Seek their advice but also critically sow the seeds in their minds that this is something you want to do as they will become your scouts and promoters.

As an example, let's return to William Eccleshare and the risk he took in leaving his highly successful 20-year career in advertising to join McKinsey. It was this decision that kicked off his non-executive career. His first NXD role was with British recruitment company Hays, which he held from 2004 to 2014, but he says that he would never even have got a foot in the door had it not been for his stint at McKinsey, which gave him the credibility as well as the network to make the appointment possible.

Inevitably, you will also need to plug yourself into the headhunter network – governance protocol around independence means that, more often than not, search firms are appointed to recruit non-executive directors. These firms will typically have a Boards Practice, so try and get to those consultants.

Also think about what the attributes are for a good board director as they are subtly different from those for a full-time executive. The first, and in many ways most important, thing is the need to be **objective and independent**. This might seem like stating the obvious, but it is much harder than you might think, in particular if you have just come out of decades in leadership roles. There will be an overwhelming desire to direct the executive team, but the clue is in the title: non-executive director. Your job is to be not only simultaneously supportive but also challenging of the executive team – a "critical friend" as a former Board Practice colleague put it. Integrity and honesty (and being unafraid to deploy those) are absolutely vital.

Next, you will need sound **commercial and financial nous**. This is not just about reading a balance sheet (though that does help), but about a holistic grasp of the business, its operating model, its value drivers, and where it sits in its marketplace; in many ways the skill sets we have previously discussed about becoming an effective CEO.

As a non-executive director, you may be asked to join because you bring a very specific skill – you are a former finance director and therefore a critical member of the Audit Committee, or a former HR director and so a contender for the Remuneration Committee. But actually you're there to bring **intellectual precision, informed self-confidence, and insight** to the discussion, without, of course, being the cleverest person in the room. You will need to leave your ego at the door.

Finally, a **genuine interest in the business/sector** also helps. Remember that your commitment as a non-executive director could be as much as nine years (three terms of three years until you are deemed to be no longer independent as defined by the UK Corporate Governance Code), not to mention a board meeting nearly every month. So all good reasons why you really need to feel interested and engaged by the business before you commit to join.

★

The CEO, the cheese shop owner, the sunseeker, and the portfolio non-executive – these are just four representative examples. But they hopefully serve as a useful exercise for executives thinking about the next stage of their life, as it personalises and makes real the output of an individual's work life and ambitions. It creates a simple context for building a roadmap to get you to your end destination.

CONCLUSION

I said right at the start that this book is not a panacea. And that's the truth. There isn't a book in the world capable of giving the right advice at the right time to every person who reads it.

But what I also said at the start is that I'd use my 40 years' experience, and the insights of some of the most successful and inspirational people I know, to offer a toolkit to help those who are thinking they need to change something.

You may have got to the end and thought you don't need to change a thing. That's great; more power to your elbow.

But for those who are looking for help, who do think they need to make a change, and who are currently at the mercy of the car in front, I hope I have offered some practical advice.

Of course change is always hard. But it is not so hard when you have the right tools. This book started as a mission to offer those tools to anyone who may want or need them. And I'd like to finish it that way too.

So rather than spending the final lines philosophising and pontificating about what I think you can take from this book or how it can influence your life, I'd like to give you something which might be genuinely practical – the key points to take away, and to always keep in mind as you make the decisions that will impact your work life, and by extension the rest of it.

Tear it out and stick it on your mirror, take a photo of it and set it as your phone background, turn this page over, and never look at it again; it's up to you. But here are the lessons I want to leave you with:

1) *Be generous to yourself.* Few executives actively manage their careers, which are typically a function of hard work, brainpower, good luck, and, only occasionally, proactive decision-making. You are not alone!
2) *Increase your rate of proactive career decisions.* Each one will have a material effect on the quality of your professional and personal life.
3) *Acknowledge the legacies and frailties of your younger self.* Don't let them define you negatively, but understand and learn from them to enhance your self-awareness. This means actively seeking feedback, embracing 360s, and seeking out a coach or mentor.
4) *Take risks.* This will need self-belief and courage. Sometimes the risk will be the right call, sometimes not. But the act of taking that risk will propel you forward in terms of improved adaptability and resilience.
5) *Approach every career junction strategically as well as emotionally.* Each time ask yourself: what do I need? What do I want? What am I good at? Evaluating every opportunity in this way will help objectify your decision.
6) *Present career achievements in terms of "How" not "What."* This will ensure you identify and amplify your Competencies. These will be the bridges to lateral career moves.
7) *Define your Personal Brand.* This is an exercise in prioritising your core attributes and then amplifying them and will help focus decision-making as well as your leadership style.
8) *Explore beyond your solar system.* Use your competencies to think which skills will be transferable to adjacent business sectors.
9) *Think in ten-year increments.* What does your life look like in ten years' time? Will your current trajectory get you there? If it doesn't, work back from that and identify the building blocks that will.
10) *If in doubt, stick this Carl Jung quote on your fridge door:* "I am not what happened to me. I am what I choose to become."

TWELVE JOURNEYS

Name: Zillah Byng-Thorne

Alma Mater: University of Glasgow

Current Role: CEO of Future PLC

Route to the Top: Byng-Thorne joined Future in 2013, so has been at the media company for the best part of a decade now. Her career previous to Future, though, was admirably diverse, with regular moves.

She began at Nestle as a graduate trainee, where she spent two years before joining HMV as a treasury analyst. At HMV, Byng-Thorne worked in the corporate office, getting greater exposure to senior management than she might otherwise have expected. As a result, she says, "I decided that I wanted to be a CFO before I was 30." So she left HMV after two years to join GE Capital – "to go and learn from the best." Despite intentions to spend a good stint at GE, a reluctance to move abroad away from her family meant she spent just over a year there before joining drinks chain Threshers in 2002. In 2004, at the age of 29, she was made CFO. Two years later, she took up the same role at Fitness First. "It was a different type of role. I thought it would really help round out my experience as a CFO and broaden my capability, so personally I thought, this is a real test of my ability, and I'll really learn from it." She wasn't wrong, but perhaps not in the way she expected.

Early on in her tenure at Fitness First, a fraud was uncovered. Byng-Thorne was sent to run the German business as managing director, alongside her CFO responsibilities. "That was my first introduction into general management in what was quite a hostile environment, because this had been the epicentre where a fraud had been committed." In a year she had the German business back in growth, she built a new team, and hired her replacement as MD. But despite her successes, she was forced out of her CFO role in 2009. "I was devastated, staggered," she says.

A former colleague recommended her for the vacant CFO job at Autotrader, which she held from 2009 to 2012, a period in which she also became a non-executive director at Mecom Group PLC and studied for a master's degree in Coaching and Behavioural Change from Henley Management College. The decision to do the latter was taken after Byng-Thorne reflected on the fallout from her time at Fitness First and decided "if I want to move my career on, I need to become less logical, and more emotional."

After leaving Autotrader in 2013 following 11 months as interim CEO, Byng-Thorne decided to go plural, joining the boards of Trainline, The Hut Group, Betfair, and the DVLA. But then Future came calling. She started as CFO on a part-time basis, allowing her to continue her non-executive career alongside. But within months, she was asked to step into the CEO role.

Since taking over as CEO of Future in 2014, she has overseen its stunning transformation from a magazine business to a global media company. Future's audience has more than tripled in the last three years. And while other publishers were taking UK government furlough at the start of the COVID-19 pandemic, Future gave all its staff £1,000 to help with the cost of home-working.

Early influence: Her parents both had strong, but different, ideologies. Mum: never rely on anyone. Dad: be the best of the best at what you do.

Pearl of Wisdom: "Be really careful what you wish for!"

★★★

Name: Stephen A. Carter

Alma Mater: University of Aberdeen

Current Role: Group Chief Executive of Informa plc

Route to the Top: Carter is not a man who could ever be accused of following the car in front. During his incredibly varied career, he has worked in both the private and public sectors. He is currently, and has been for nearly the last decade, group chief executive of FTSE 100 company Informa.

A self-professed "career entrepreneur," Carter studied law at the University of Aberdeen. He did not, though, become a practising Scottish lawyer but "went to the next best thing, which was commercial advocacy"; also known as advertising. Carter joined J Walter Thompson as a graduate trainee in 1986. Inside a decade, he was running the show as chief executive.

In 2000, he joined NTL (now Virgin Media) as managing director, and then chief operating officer. He left after leading the UK company as the US group and holding company went through a complex refinancing and US bankruptcy protection process. Of his move to NTL, Carter says: "It probably turned out to be the most challenging experience of my career then, and possibly now. Whatever beyond my experience was then, I was beyond it. However, I could not begin to explain all the things that I learned during that first technology boom and bust, and it has served me very well."

In March 2003, Carter became the founding CEO of UK media regulator Ofcom. "I had always had a public service interest and was ready for a change, a different drumbeat," he says. "At Ofcom we had the opportunity to create something new and different that was the best of the public sector (purpose, robustly independent, and long term) and the best of the private sector (high quality, efficient, effective, and agile)."

In January 2008, Carter became UK Prime Minister Gordon Brown's chief of strategy and principal adviser. Then subsequently, by entering the House of Lords as Lord Carter of Barnes, he became the Minister for Communications and Technology. As minister, he commissioned and largely wrote the Digital Britain report and the subsequent legislation, the Digital Economy Act 2010.

After leaving Government, Carter was privately advised by a mentor, the former SABMiller chief executive Graham Mackay, "to leave the UK, get back into business, and stay away for longer than the official cooling off period." So he moved to Paris at the end of 2009 to join Alcatel-Lucent, where he became CEO of the European businesses and chief marketing officer.

On moving to the French capital, Carter reflects: "If you want a humbling and developmental experience in the middle of your professional life, move to a different city. Work in an industry you have never worked in, in a language you speak only averagely, know almost nobody, and almost nobody will know you. Particularly helpful when you have just come from a place where you have some established credibility and reputation and some or most people will take your call! It was a great experience and I wish I had done it earlier."

Carter joined the board of Informa as a non-executive director in 2010 and three years later was approached by the board to consider applying for the group CEO role. Carter was successfully appointed as group chief executive in 2013. At the time, the company was domiciled in Switzerland, but in 2014, he returned the senior management team and the Informa company domicile to the UK.

Early Influence: Carter is clear on this: "Education, Education, Education. My time at university was formative in so many ways. Learning, lifelong friendships, deep involvement in student affairs and student politics, a degree, which both suited and stimulated me. I got so much out of it, I stayed for five years."

Pearl of Wisdom: "The key is to know something that no one else knows. It doesn't really matter what you choose, as long as it captures your interest and your imagination. Find something you're going to be more knowledgeable about than many of those around you."

★★★

Name: Roger Davis

Alma Mater: University of Oxford

Current Role: Chairman of Bupa

Route to the Top: Davis wanted to be a soldier like his father from an early age. So when he left school, he went to the Royal Military Academy Sandhurst, where he was commissioned into the Royal Tank Regiment and encouraged to apply for an in-service degree at Oxford.

He left the British Army shortly after his 30th birthday in 1986 and joined Robert Fleming Holdings as an equity sales manager, eventually rising to become managing director of India at Jardine Fleming by the mid-1990s.

In 1996, he moved to Hong Kong after being lured to BZW, the now defunct Barclays investment banking arm, to be CEO of Asia Pacific. According to Davis, this was "a bit like going down to the park on Sunday and saying to the No. 9, 'Do you want to start for Manchester United next Saturday?'" But it was "the piece of luck I needed, and I knew I could do it."

In 2001, he returned to the UK all set to leave Barclays before being asked to run Barclays UK. He did eventually leave four years later, aged 49, having said to his wife, "when I get to 50, I will probably stop full-time work."

If stopping full-time work was the plan, it may have failed, as Davis has since built an enviable non-executive career. But he admits things did not start so well when he "hit a snake rather than a ladder" investing in an aerospace parts business that turned out to be built on sand. He has since been Chairman of Sainsbury's Bank, between 2013 and 2020, and a non-executive director of global information services company Experian for 12 years.

Davis was appointed Bupa Chairman in 2018. "When I decided to take the portfolio route," he says, "I knew I wanted to end up with a large global business of which I would be chairman."

"I've now ended up exactly where I had hoped to be. I'm chairman of Bupa, which is a multibillion global business, and which I really love."

Early influence: Davis says that overhearing his father "almost pleading" with an Italian shopkeeper to buy back some camping gas cylinders so he could afford the petrol to get home drove him, from an early age, to succeed and "make some money."

Pearl of Wisdom: "You learn a lot more from the bad times than you do from the good times."

★★★

Name: William Eccleshare

Alma Mater: Trinity College, University of Cambridge

Current Role: Worldwide CEO of Clear Channel Outdoor Holdings

Route to the Top: Eccleshare readily admits to following the car in front early in his career, and a look at his CV backs that up. He joined J Walter Thompson as a graduate trainee in 1978 and would remain there for 17 years. He was fast-tracked through the ranks of JWT, and "I didn't really think beyond that *Campaign* headline that said: William Eccleshare Appointed MD of JWT London." It didn't quite work out like that, because in 1992, he was asked to go and run JWT in Amsterdam. "It wasn't where I had seen myself," he says, "it was a moment of great disappointment. But it turned out to be the best thing that could possibly happen." Because, Eccleshare explains, it was the first time he hadn't got the next move he expected and he realised that he wasn't in control of his career.

So, after three years in Amsterdam, Eccleshare finally left JWT to become CEO of Ammirati Puris Lintas. "The opportunity to run a London agency was still an itch that I felt I needed to scratch," he says, "and although it was one of the most enjoyable experiences of my career it didn't really stretch me intellectually, and it did nothing for my career story."

Feeling that he had learnt all he could from an advertising industry which wasn't going anywhere fast, in 2000 Eccleshare got out altogether and joined McKinsey as a partner and leader of European Branding Practice. "I was very conscious of it as a way of stretching myself, of learning and of opening up possibilities," he says. "It was no fun at all!" But it was the two and a half years Eccleshare spent at McKinsey that laid the groundwork for the next stage of his career, not least because it was during that time he got his first non-executive director role at Hays.

Eccleshare's ambition for his next step at that point was to run a business, "but it didn't feel to me it was going to be easy in one hop." But in a few hops. . . ?

He returned to the advertising industry in 2002 as the chairman and chief executive of Y&R Europe and was then CEO of BBDO in Europe between 2006 and 2009. But again he got the feeling of not being in control of his own destiny. "I couldn't see what the next step was. And I wanted to run a business of scale." Enter Clear Channel. Eccleshare joined the billboards group in 2009 as CEO of Clear Channel International, and was made CEO of Clear Channel Outdoor Holdings in 2012. He is now worldwide CEO of Clear Channel Outdoor Holdings and fulfilled a personal ambition by taking the company public and ringing the opening bell at NYSE.

Early influence: On a family bereavement when he was 11, Eccleshare says: "The death of my eldest sister certainly formed me in making me grow up very quickly and want to take control of my life. I think it made me, during my secondary school, very focused on what I was going to do to escape from what had become a very sad and difficult family life in a way."

Pearl of Wisdom: "Take some risks and do something different. Think about your career as a series of experiences that you're going to learn from and want to look back on and be able to make some sense out of."

★★★

Name: June Felix

Alma Mater: University of Pittsburgh

Current Role: CEO at IG Group plc

Route to the Top: Felix has been CEO of trading platform IG since 2018. Her CV is impressive to say the least. It includes stints at Procter & Gamble, Johnson and Johnson, Booz Allen Hamilton, Deutsche Bank, Chase Manhattan, IBM, and Citibank. Perhaps this is not a surprise for someone whose "burning ambition" led her to finish top of her class at university. "I had one B in four years of studying chemical engineering and pre-med," Felix reveals.

But an executive career was not always the plan. "I wanted to get into med school," Felix says. However, after working in a hospital as a blood collector, she decided medicine was not for her. "It really made me feel like I couldn't do this," she says. "Because it was so enervating . . . It's just working against really difficult odds. And I just thought I would have to become such a callous person if I did this every day."

So instead she started her career at P&G before moving to Johnson and Johnson in 1979. Five years later, it was onto Booz Allen. Throughout the 1990s, Felix worked for Chase before she became chief executive of financial cryptography startup Certco in 2000. "I joined in January 2000, and a couple of months after I got there, of course, the dotcom bubble burst." She managed to complete a fairly impressive salvage job, but the company was eventually wound up. It was on to IBM, where she ran the banking and financial markets industry sector. "I had teams all over the world," Felix says, "so, I lived on a plane for seven years."

Not wanting to continue that intense lifestyle – "I was travelling 75 percent of the time" – Felix ran global healthcare at Citi Enterprise Payments, a division of Citibank, between 2010 and 2014 before becoming president of Europe and Russia for Verifone, one of the world's largest point-of-sale terminal vendors. "It was a hardware piece. I'd never sold a hardware piece, I knew nothing about hardware until that moment," she says. And it was her first time living in Europe.

Four years later, she became CEO of IG, a company she had first become involved with in 2015 when she was appointed a non-executive director. "What I loved about IG is it was a global platform business, international focus, technology, but direct to consumer; very edgy, innovative company. It sounded great." She wasn't wrong.

Early influence: Felix says her family influenced and supported her in many ways. Raised as a Christian, she had an ethos embedded in her that "if you have any gifts, make the most of them." She was also spurred on by seeing her brilliant mother "never really reaching her full potential because women weren't supposed to in her generation."

Pearl of Wisdom: "Always raise your hand"

★★★

Name: Alan Jope

Alma Mater: University of Edinburgh

Current Role: Chief Executive of Unilever

Route to the Top: Jope's inclusion here may seem unexpected given he is a one-company man. How can someone, you might ask, who is now at the head of the same multinational company he joined as a graduate trainee in 1985, be a good example of not following the car in front? Well, in his own words, "climbing the ladder was absolutely never an objective." And that is played out when examining Jope's progress through Unilever, where he has consistently taken on unexpected, unglamorous, often risky roles that eventually made him a prime candidate for the top job.

Jope almost never joined Unilever at all. After studying a business degree at the University of Edinburgh – a last-minute change after initially being accepted for medicine – he agreed to become an auditor at Arthur Andersen. But another late-in-the-day change-of-heart saw him apply to Unilever and Procter & Gamble. He got an offer from both, joining the former after his "then-girlfriend, now wife, discovered P&G were in Newcastle and Unilever were in central London." After a few more conventional trainee rotations at the company, he accepted a Midlands sales role in large part because the job came with a car, "and I actually ended up running a quarter of the UK with 10 guys working for me." Five years into his time at Unilever, Jope asked to be sent to Southeast Asia. Instead, he was sent to New York to be the brand manager of the hand and nail variant of Vaseline. "It was an unglamorous job," he says, "but I got stuck into it and after six months was put in charge of all of Vaseline, which was actually the biggest brand in the company."

Jope was eventually granted his wish to go to southeast Asia, taking up a "very ambiguous job" in Thailand that, again turned into a much-expanded role. He returned to the U.S. in 1999 to help integrate Helene Curtis into Unilever. Two years later, in his mid-30s, Jope was made President of Unilever's Home & Personal Care business in North America, a job "way beyond my capability or experience." In 2009, Jope was then asked to lead Unilever's business in China, a role he describes as "a notorious departure lounge . . . the previous six general managers of Unilever China had moved on at the end of the assignment." At least in part down to a desire to broaden the horizons of his children, Jope took the role, doubled the size of the business, and laid the foundations for its further success. "That was probably the assignment that put me in the role that I'm in right now." He succeeded Paul Polman as Unilever CEO in January 2019.

Early influence: "An absolute intolerance of whinging," instilled in him by his parents and a schoolboy rugby coach, gave Jope an independent-mindedness and resourcefulness that has served him well in his career.

Pearl of Wisdom: "I do believe gathering breadth of experience is important. Trying the alternative, trying the thing that no one else wants to try, especially early on. So whether it's taking the job in sales, when everyone else is going into marketing, or taking the kind of unglamorous brand job to get an interesting country experience, or going to China when everyone gets sacked at the end of that."

★★★

Name: Guy Laurence

Alma Mater: Teesside Polytechnic

Current Role: Chief executive of Chelsea Football Club

Route to the Top: If there's a phrase that sums up Laurence's career, it's this: "And then I looked left and right." Whenever he has felt he might be following the car in front, he has looked for alternatives and found a new route.

Laurence enjoyed business success while still at school, building a candle-making company within the Young Enterprise programme. At Teesside Polytechnic (now Teesside University), he managed part of the student business operations and built them out (which included opening a new 311-bedroom campus). Due to his role running many of the student bars, he realised the potential of arcade machines. Aged 21, he wrote to Chris Wright, the owner of Chrysalis Records, the biggest jukebox operator in the UK, telling him arcade machines were the next big thing. Laurence was duly hired by Chrysalis and never went back to university.

He subsequently joined Grand Met (a forerunner of Diageo), where he moved into marketing. At 30, he decided he needed to learn how to run a company, so he went to work with a friend who had a nationwide specialist cleaning company. "The industry was dull as dishwater," he says, "but I learnt a lot about running companies." He then moved into the film industry, first in marketing for multiplex cinemas, then on the studio side working for MGM. A foray into the restaurant business with themed chain Planet Hollywood followed – "a catastrophic mistake" – before a stint with pay-TV service ONdigital.

All of which led him into the dotcom world with Vizzavi, which was later acquired by Vodafone, where he really made his name. From 2002 to 2005, he was chief executive of Vizzavi and then group product director for Vodafone. In 2005, he became chief executive of Vodafone Netherlands. He became chief executive of Vodafone UK in 2008. And in 2013, he became president and CEO of Rogers Communications, the largest mobile and cable operator in Canada. "They had mobile, TV, media, and sports," explains Laurence. "I knew all the business except sports, so in the evenings I spent time learning how to run sports teams." It would pay major dividends as, after being ousted from Rogers Communications in 2016, Laurence eventually took over in the Chelsea top job in 2018.

Early influence: Laurence's father was an entrepreneur who enjoyed varying success. As a result, Laurence says, his family went from big houses, to small houses across the country. This also meant he moved school a lot. "I went through quite a bit of difficult change in my early years," he says, "which really equipped me to deal with change as an adult."

Pearl of Wisdom: "The only constant is change."

★★★

Name: Jonathan Lewis

Alma Mater: Kingston University London

Current Role: CEO of Capita

Route to the Top: Unusually for the head of a public company, Lewis started his career with a decade in academia. Despite "completely flunking" his A-levels, he got a place at Kingston Polytechnic (now Kingston University London) in 1981 to study geology, and after becoming passionate about the subject, went on to a PhD at Reading University. "I literally went from being a C-class student in the sixth form," he says, "to being very knowledgeable about a very small area of scientific knowledge."

A research fellowship at Imperial College London followed, before a move to Edinburgh's Heriot-Watt University. Throughout his academic career, Lewis was consulting for global oil and gas companies, and he eventually joined Texas-based software and technology company Landmark in 1996 (shortly before it was acquired by Halliburton). "It was an informed decision to transition to the commercial world," Lewis says, "I'd decided there was only so much more I could do in academia. I'd be doing the same thing for the rest of my life. And I didn't want to do that."

Landmark was a "fantastic training ground in a very fast moving sector," says Lewis. In 2006, he moved to Halliburton proper when asked to repair the American behemoth's "completely broken relationship" with Exxon Mobil. A run of successes at the company saw Lewis elevated to Halliburton's executive committee, but he eventually lost out to Jeff Miller for the job of CEO in the mid-2010s. "It was, without doubt, the most disappointing event of my career before or since."

So after a decade at Halliburton, Lewis left in 2016. "I was content with working for Halliburton," he says, "and in some ways it would have been the easier path." But instead he came back to the UK to become CEO of Amec Foster Wheeler, which he returned to profitability before selling to Wood Group for £2.2 billion in 2017.

Having earned "this reputation for being a turnaround guy," he was then approached for the role he currently holds, that of Capita CEO, which he filled in December 2017.

Early influence: Lewis says being an adopted child and moving from London to the small Welsh mining town in which he grew up armed him with the resilience that has been a fundamental part of his success.

Pearl of Wisdom: "If you cannot handle disappointment, you just won't have the resilience to get through it."

★★★

Name: Gavin Patterson

Alma Mater: Emmanuel College, University of Cambridge

Current Role: President and Chief Revenue Officer of Salesforce

Route to the Top: Patterson's career journey started in a sector which, for many, has been an important academy for later success – the world of consumer packaged goods. In this case, it was Procter & Gamble which, in the 1990s, became a factory for high-performing talent because the company's training and development of brand managers groomed them for later general management.

He spent nine years at P&G, working alongside the likes of Tim Davie, now Director General of the BBC, and current BT CEO Philip Jansen. He was the marketing director by 1996 and eventually left for cable company Telewest (now part of Virgin Media) in 1999.

Jansen played a key role in Patterson joining Telewest, just as he had done a decade earlier for P&G, when the pair met at a careers stand at Cambridge. "Phil came across me wandering around Cambridge in a cricket sweatshirt, and he started talking to me because he loves cricket," says Patterson. "I listened to him for a bit and then pointed out I don't play cricket at all. This was a jumper I would wear from a fashion perspective!" The rest, as they say, is history.

Patterson describes his four years at Telewest as "turbulent" – not least because of the dot-com bubble bursting in 2000 – but says it was an "extraordinary learning experience" that played a key role in his progress. "I had this huge burst of experience that took me from being a marketing director to a general manager. And then BT called."

Patterson was appointed managing director of BT Group's consumer division in January 2004. He joined the board aged 39 and was eventually appointed as CEO, replacing Ian Livingston, in 2013. After "a good stint" of five and half years in the top job at BT, Patterson left in January 2019. His replacement was Philip Jansen.

"For the first six months after I finished at BT," Patterson says, "I'd concluded that I didn't want to do another executive job and I'd go plural." However, he was tempted back into the fray by Salesforce founder Marc Benioff. It was a slow burn, with Patterson initially working just a day a week for the Silicon Valley software giant before he realised, "at 51, I was too young to stop."

Early influence: Being a middle-class boy in a tough comprehensive taught him resilience but also that being a good sportsman was a critical leveller.

Pearl of Wisdom: "Life is too short to work with people that don't share your values. Work with great people, both internally and externally. And where you've got a choice, and people have a lot more choice than they think they do sometimes, exercise it."

★★★

Name: John Smith

Alma Mater: University of Life

Current Role: Portfolio

Route to the Top: Smith started his career aged 15, immediately after taking his O-levels. He had wanted to be an architect, an aspiration fuelled by a childhood love of Lego and Meccano, but the need for a seven-year degree made that dream a non-starter. An aptitude for maths, though, led him into an accountancy firm, where he began his qualifications "on a day-release basis" before joining the British Railways Board in the mid-1970s. Soon after joining the BRB, Smith was accepted onto their fast-track management development programme, a three-year scheme that allowed him to complete his accountancy qualifications while also being trained in all aspects of management and leadership across a number of different jobs. "It was an amazing privilege to be on such a thing," Smith says. He subsequently played a key role in the sale of many of the BRB's non railway-related businesses – ferry services, hotels, engineering works, and coffee shops – that took place while Margaret Thatcher was prime minister in the 1980s.

Smith was duly headhunted by the BBC and joined as group chief accountant in 1989, a decision he hails as hugely significant for the rest of his career, which he has spent on the borderline between creativity and business. "I'd entered a company that was really close to all my passions," he says, "I loved everything about it." As a result of being "interested in everything, not just the finance," Smith mutated (his word) into the BBC's COO, a role he took on in 2000. In that role, his architectural aspirations were realised as he oversaw huge building projects for the corporation, including the renovation of the iconic Broadcasting House.

In 2004, Smith was appointed CEO of BBC Worldwide – "that is the moment where my career took off." A relatively small, dormant company when Smith took over, he transformed the business, doubling BBC Worldwide's turnover and quadrupling its profits. Smith's eight-year tenure saw the launch of BBC.com, as well as BBC Worldwide's international production business, which produced successful TV formats like Top Gear and Dancing with the Stars.

He joined the board of Burberry as a non-executive director in 2009 and became the luxury fashion company's COO in 2013 after leaving the BBC. He held that role until 2017, when he opted to go plural. On taking the portfolio route rather than another executive position – he had been offered a couple of CEO roles – Smith concludes: "It's a scary moment. Because suddenly you've got financial uncertainty, and what-do-you-do-each-day uncertainty, and your sense of purpose is suddenly rather different. But my God, I'd never look back."

Early influence: Smith says he has been heavily influenced by two key things: his mother's attitude to parenting ("just make sure you're back before the sun goes down") – which made for an "incredibly happy" childhood – and a desire never to struggle for money as his parents had to. "Those two things, of being completely free and being able to get into anything, on the one hand," he says, "and being driven by a desire not to be poor again, have essentially driven my entire life since then."

Pearl of Wisdom: "It's your beliefs and interests that should guide you, not thinking about the next step."

★★★

Name: Melanie Smith

Alma Mater: University of Auckland

Current Role: CEO of Ocado Retail

Route to the Top: To say that Smith does not fit the mould of a typical CEO would be something of an understatement. Her tough childhood culminated in her leaving home at 16. But that did not prevent her from finishing her high school education (at a school where she was the only Maori) before going to the University of Auckland to study law and commerce. "I went to university," Smith says, "because I didn't want to end up mowing lawns or working in a supermarket, and I sure as fuck didn't want to be poor."

Out of university, rather than moving into law, Smith joined McKinsey, led by a desire to be a decision-maker, but even more importantly, to travel the world. After a tricky start at the consultancy giants – "I wasn't very good at the job, I didn't have the toolkit" – Smith remained there for over a decade, during which time she was elected partner.

In 2009, Smith swapped the relentlessness of McKinsey for TalkTalk. "It was a mistake in hindsight because I didn't know the industry," she says. "I learned a ton in the 18 months I was there but it probably wasn't my wisest career choice." A stint as a freelance consultant followed before she was persuaded to join Bupa in 2013, where she spent three years doing "all the jobs."

And then, Smith retired, as she describes it, and travelled more of the world. But she was lured back to work in 2017 when she joined Marks and Spencer as strategy director. It was at M&S that she negotiated the £750 million joint venture with Ocado. Despite this, though, when the job of Ocado Retail CEO came up, Smith "wasn't even in consideration for it." Despite that particular obstacle, she got the job in August 2019.

"I think I got it because of my drive and energy," she concludes. "I do things in an unusual way [but] I'd rather get fired for trying to do it the way I want to do it than get fired for doing it the way someone else told me to."

Early influence: Smith says that her tough upbringing in New Zealand gave her huge drive and resilience as well as a knowledge of what it's like to have no money. She adds: "I'm really lucky, one of the things about coming from a poor family is I'm really frugal. So it means if I get fired tomorrow, I'm good."

Pearl of Wisdom: "If you look after the smart people, they will keep coming back to work for you."

***

Name: Stevie Spring

Alma Mater: University of Kent

Current Role: Chairman of the British Council and Mind

Route to the Top: Route to the Top: Spring describes herself as having had a twin-track career from the age of 16. "I have always," she says, "had a commercial job and a not-for-profit one in parallel."

She initially wanted to be a PE teacher but was persuaded to go to Kent University to study law with a view to becoming a barrister. Instead, Spring left university and stumbled into a marketing career at James Gulliver Associates, before moving to TV-am and then joining Grey Group in 1984.

"I took to advertising like a duck to water, because I think the law is great training for advertising – being an advocate for products and services instead of people," she says. So it would prove as she went from Grey Group to Gold Greenlees Trott to WMGO before joining the management team at Y&R in 1994.

In 2000, she was appointed chief executive of outdoor advertising company Clear Channel UK, a job she says she was ready for "after 30 years of serving – and learning – on not-for-profit boards." And six and a half years later, she became CEO of British media company Future. "I went to Future because, regardless of sector, I really wanted to try my hand at running a public company," Spring says.

It was during her time at Future that Spring became chairman of BBC Children in Need having served three terms as chair of the Groundwork Federation. And it was when Spring left Future in 2012 that she truly went plural because, she says, "as an ex PLC CEO (or CFO), there are more opportunities for non exec roles."

She is currently chairman of the British Council, the UK's international organisation for arts, culture, and education, as well as mental health charity Mind. She is a non-executive director and chairman of remuneration for the Cooperative Group, and is an investor/advisor to two technology companies.

Early influence: Spring credits her father, who was a single parent and worked for the railways, with giving her and her sister "a very rounded cultural education" and "a very strong moral compass." The former was developed by the trips her family would take to "go and see anything that was free" by train with their free rail passes. The latter from the family board meetings, instigated by her father when Spring was seven, during which broad social issues were debated under AOB.

Pearl of Wisdom: "Respond to opportunities in the moment. Just because you haven't doesn't mean you can't."

INDEX

Adelman, Sophie 53
Advanced Management Programme (AMP) 75
advertising 2–3, 8, 13, 37, 55–56, 86, 89, 95, 98
Advertising Standards Authority 75
advisory work 55
affiliation professional identity 68
Airbnb 21
Amazon Prime 54
ambition 13–14; professional identity 68
Ammirati Puris Lintas 6
AMV BBDO 13
archetype(s) 65–69; branding you and 65, 66–69; drivers of 68; Haines McGregor wheel of 66–67; hero 66; Jung concept of 65–66
Arts Council England 26
ASOS 27
Atlantic, The 22
atychiphobia 33; *see also* failure
authenticity, social media use and 81–82
AutoScout24 30
Awa, Winnie 25, 27, 33
awards/citations, CV 62

baby boomers 20
Bazalgette, Peter 26–27
BBC Worldwide 6, 26, 73

Beckett, Samuel 35
"become respectable," networking and 74–75
being yourself, women and 12–13
Berger, Edgar 30
Berkeley Well-Being Institute, The 34
Biden, Joe 20
Blackett, Karen 12, 14–15
Botin, Ana 83
brand: archetypes and 65, 66–69; personal 92; social media and 81
British Council and Mind 30
British Gas 86
Brittain, Alison 11
Brown, Gordon 33
Bupa 13, 35
Burberry 73
Burkus, David 72–73
Bush, George W. 25
Bushism, defined 25
Business in the Community 13
Business Leader (magazine) 11
Business School rankings, 2021 75–76
business/sector interest, NXD and 90
Byng-Thorne, Zillah 76; journey of 93–94

capabilities 8, 32, 51, 82
capital needs 88

Capita plc 30, 47
career decisions: fixed mindset and 5–7; increase rate of proactive 92; midlife caution and 7
career history, CV 62
career progression 7, 17, 20–21, 30, 92
careers: changing, timing for 51–52; generations and 19–22
career strategies 20, 92
Carra 25, 33
Carter, Stephen A. 6, 33; journey of 94–96
Chelsea Football Club 87
chief executive (CE) 85
Clear Channel 6
Clifton, Rita 16
Clubhouse 83
coaches/coaching 46, 47, 73, 76, 92
collective unconscious, archetypes and 65
Collett Dickenson & Pearce 1
comfort zone 31
commercial/financial nous NXD 90
Communications Store, The 27
community engagement 81
competencies 55, 92; CV and 57–62; definitions of 58; factors of focus for 59, 60–61; job sectors and, exploring 62–64; key, for CV 62; professional identity wheel applied to 68; structuring 61–62
confidence issues 16–17
Crozier, Adam 54
cul-de-sac executives 7–9
curriculum vitae (CV) 57–62; competencies and 57–62; described 58; exploring job sectors and 62–64; structuring 61–62; turning, inside out 59; what vs. how component of 58
CV see curriculum vitae (CV)

Davie, Tim 6, 7
Davis, Roger 35; journey of 96–97
Davis, Tchiki 34
Day, Elizabeth 34

Demon-Haunted World, The (Sagan) 38
Dexter, Julietta 27
Dunning, David 43
Dunning-Kruger effect 43–44
Dweck, Carol 5, 35

eBay 22
Eccleshare, William 6, 89; journey of 97–99
education: coaching 76, 94; CV 62; networking and 75–76
Endemol Shine Group 12
endgame 85–90; capital needs 88; leadership role strategy/tactics 85–88; non-executive roles 88–90; overview 85
enjoyment 49, 50
entrepreneur(s) 25–28; adventure route of 26–27; French word origin of 25; hats worn by 27; as risk-takers 26, 28
Epic of Gilgamesh 66
Ernst & Young 27
experience, diversity of 31

Facebook 13, 21, 71, 79, 83
failure: exercise in looking at 34; resilience and 35; success and 33–36
faking it 16–17
family, work and 15
Federer, Roger 51
feedback, seeking 44–45, 46
Felix, June 85; journey of 99–100
Fels, Anna 13–14
Financial Times 75
Financial Times Effective Non-Executive Director Programme 88
first job 29–30
fixed mindset 5–7; defined 5; executive interviews pertaining to 6–7; following the car in front and 5–6; vs. growth 5
Football Association 86
Founders Factory 25

Four Dimensional Executive Assessment process (KF4D-Exec) 59
Friend of a Friend . . . Understanding the Hidden Networks That Can Transform Your Life and Your Career (Burkus) 72–73
Frot-Coutaz, Cecile 13
functional skill set, going beyond 86
functional tourist 86
Future plc 76

Gadhia, Jayne-Anne 15
Garden, The 53
Garfield, Liv 11, 12, 13, 14
Gates, Bill 20
Geluck, Philippe 43
generations: careers and 19–22; differences in workplace 20; 2008 global financial crisis and 21–22; work environment and 20
generous to yourself 92
Gen X 20
Gen Z 20
"get known" networking advice 73–74
GlaxoSmithKline 11
Glenn, Martin 86
global financial crisis, 2008 21–22
Gold Greenlees Trott 7
good, success and being 49, 50–51
Gooding, Val 13, 14
Gray, Thomas 44
Group M 12
growth mindset: defined 5; executive interviews pertaining to 6–7; *vs.* fixed 5

habits, social media use and 81
Haines, Jeremy 65
Haines McGregor wheel of archetypes 65, 66–67
Harrison, Tristia 12
Harvard Business Review 13, 38, 46
Hays 89
headhunter 57, 59, 86, 89

Heineken 87
hero archetype 66
Hoberman, Brent 25
Hogarth, Peter 73
How To Fail (podcast) 34
Hudack, Caroline 21, 52

IG Group plc 85
Igloo 86
Ikigai 49–51
Impala 21, 52
independent board director 90
Informa plc 6, 33
informed self-confidence, NXD and 90
Ingram, Tamara 12, 14
insight, NXD and 90
Instagram 83
intellect professional identity 68
intellectual precision, NXD and 90
Interbrand 16
interview narrative 59
ITV 11, 26, 54

jobs: changing, timing for 51–52; open minds and searching for 56–57; panic and changing 56; systematic searches for 57
job sectors, exploring 62–64
Jope, Alan 30, 31; journey of 100–102
Jung, Carl 65–66, 92; *see also* archetype(s)
JWT (WPP plc) 33

Kennedy, John F. 44
key competencies, CV 62
key points/lessons learned 92
Kingston Polytechnic 58
Korn Ferry 59, 68, 73
Kruger, Justin 43
Kyriacou, Maria 12–13

Laing, Sophie Turner 12, 14, 15, 16–17
Lastminute.com 25

Laurence, Guy 87–88; journey of 102–103
Lazear, Edward 27
leadership role strategies/tactics 85–88
learning, being yourself and 13–14
Le Chat (comic strip) 43
Lewis, Dave 54
Lewis, Jonathan 30, 47, 58–59; journey of 103–104
Lewis, Michael 35
life and death axis 67
LinkedIn 80, 82–83
listening 39–40
longevity 21
Lowrey, Annie 22
Lucas, George 68

Mackenzie, Amanda 13, 14
man, ages of: cul-de-sac executives 7–9; fixed mindset 5–7; midlife caution 7
MAOA-L gene 26
McCall, Carolyn 11
McKinsey 6, 39, 89
McMillon, Doug 83
Media Practice 56
Mendelsohn, Nicola 13
mentors 46, 87–88
midlife caution 7
millennials 20, 21
Moneyball (Lewis) 35
mosaic career 30–31
Mullaney, Craig 80–82
Musk, Elon 20

name/contact details, CV 61
narrative, interview 59
Nasard, Alexis 87
needs 49, 50, 88
Net-A-Porter 27
Netflix 54
networking 71–76; *see also* social media; advice 72–73; "become respectable" examples of 74–75; Burkus on redefining 72–73; education and 75–76; "get known" advice using 73–74; overview of 71–72; "widen your circle" described 74
non-executive directorships (NXD) 88–90; attributes of 90; careers, building 89; CV 62; Eccleshare example 89; headhunter networks and 89
non-executive roles 88–90
NTL 33
NXD *see* non-executive directorships (NXD)

objective board director 90
Ocado Retail 35
Ofcom 33
office politics: dealing with 37–38; success and 36–38
open minds, job searching and 56–57
opportunity, social media and 80
Orr, Will 86

pan-business initiatives 87
panic, changing jobs and 56
Patterson, Gavin 6, 29; journey of 104–105
Pelosi, Nancy 20
people, integrate/confederate groups of 87
people factor, competencies and 59, 60
PepsiCo 6, 86
personal brand 92
personal profile, CV 61
pretending, woman and 16–17
Procter & Gamble 6
professional identity 67, 68, 81
professional journey 3
public company 85, 89

qualifications, CV 58, 62
questions: asking 38–40; follow-up 40; length of 40; listening and 39–40; *vs.* statements 40

INDEX

Rainey, M. T. 15
Rapinoe, Megan 20
references, CV 62
resilience 31, 35, 46, 92
results factor, competencies and 59, 60
risk 7; failure and 33–36
risk-taking/takers 7, 28, 92; capital need and 88; in career choices 29; entrepreneurs as 26; genetics and 32; personality traits 32; success and 32–33; women *vs.* men 32
Rose, Alison 11
Royal Bank of Scotland Group 11
Ryan, Michelle 32

Sagan, Carl 38
Salesforce 6
Santander 83
ScienceMagic.Inc. 27
self-appraisal 44
self-awareness 43–47; Dunning-Kruger effect 43–44; feedback and, seeking 44–45, 46; 360-degree reviews and 45–46
self-factor, competencies and 59, 60–61
Severn Trent plc 11, 12
sigmoid curve 52–54
Silent Generation 19
skill set, going beyond functional 86
Sky Studios 13
Smith, George 66
Smith, John 73–75, 76; journey of 105–107
Smith, Melanie 35; journey of 107–108
Snapchat 69, 84
Snoop (app) 15
Snowball, Cilla 13, 17
social media 79–84; effective use of 80–82; executive usefulness of 80; Mullaney advice on use of 80–82; platforms 82–84; reasons for using 79–80
social networking sites 79
Stuart, Spencer 56

sponsor(s) 14, 15
Spring, Stevie 30, 51; journey of 108–109
Sreenivasan, Sree 80
strategy/finance discussions, contributions to 87
success 29–40; asking questions and 38–40; career path and 30; comfort zone and 31; diversity of experience and 31; failure and 33–36; first job and 29–30; mosaic career and 30–31; office politics and 36–38; overview of 29; risk-taking and 32–33
support network building 14–15
support professional identity 68
systematic job searches 57

TalkTalk 12
Telewest 6
ten-year increments, thinking in 92
Tesco 54
thought factor, competencies and 59, 60
360-degree review 45–46
Thunberg, Greta 20
TikTok 69, 84
Times Newspapers Ltd. 86
Timms, Carrie 71
transferable skills 55, 58, 59
2021 Connected Leadership report (Brunswick) 79
Twitter 83
2008 global financial crisis 21–22

Unilever 30, 31
United Biscuits 86
"Unskilled and Unaware of It" (Kruger and Dunning) 43–44

ViacomCBS Networks International 12
Virgin Money 15

Walmart 83
Walmsley, Emma 11

warrior gene 26
WhatsApp 79
Whitbread 11
"widen your circle" networking 74
Williams, Eve 22
Winfrey, Oprah 20
Witherspoon, Reese 20
woman, ages of 11–17; ambition and 13–14; equality at CEO level 11; keep learning 13–14; overview of 11–12; pretending and 16–17; support network building 14–15
work-life balance 15

young professionals: career progression and 7; legacies/frailties of, acknowledge 92; risk-taking and 7
Yousafzai, Malala 20
YouTube 79

Zuckerberg, Mark 20